VALUE FOR VALUE

Confessions of an Itinerant Fundraiser

P. Burke Keegan

PARTNERS PRESS
Corte Madera, California

VALUE FOR VALUE

Confessions of an Itinerant Fundraiser

A Partners Press Book
Published by Partners Press
Copyright © 1990 by P. Burke Keegan

ISBN: 0-9628061-0-2

Cover Design: Hope Frank & Associates
Text Design: Beverly Galley
Typesetting: Elephant Graphics, San Francisco

First Partners Press Edition: November 1990

I dedicate this book to CT:
my rock,
my clown,
my eternal inspiration.

Table of Contents

INTRODUCTION

Value for Value: Confessions of an Itinerant Fundraiser

INTRODUCTION

I once gave a midterm exam and asked the questions: What is the responsibility of the community to an arts organization? What is that organization's responsibility to the community? My class, graduate students in an Arts Administration M.B.A. program, took me totally by surprise. Most of them responded that it is the community's responsibility to give money to support their institutions, and it is the institution's responsibility to provide popular art forms.

This suggests that arts organizations are selling widgets to eager buyers; that it is their job to figure out which widget the community wants and then produce it. The right formula or design of widget and we'll all be rich. It also seems that the community isn't getting it: here they have a responsibility to give but they're not coming forward with their checks. ORCHESTRAS ARE FOLDING, THEATERS GOING DARK ALL OVER THE COUNTRY. What's going wrong?

The struggle to understand the roles played by non-profit organizations of every shape and size in relation to the community is the central issue facing non-profits today. It affects fundraising, public relations, board development, volunteer management, program development and long range planning. I have worked with non-profit organizations as a staff member, volunteer, board member, and consultant. I have seen a variety of approaches to dealing, or not dealing, with this central struggle.

Some non-profits elect to use the doom approach. They are sure that the community will never understand them, let alone love them, so they shake their collective fists at the world and struggle along into obscurity. Some non-profits approach the community with arrogance: "We're doing the really important work and if you were responsible you'd give us money." Yet others try the hat-in-hand approach, grateful for any crumbs that fall their way. I have seen some non-profits so afraid of going to people for money that they spend **years** coming up with excuses for why "It wouldn't work anyway."

The non-profit organizations that prosper have come to grips with how they relate to their community. They fundraise appropriately, involve key people in their work, thank people well and thoughtfully, attract media attention, and hold a proud place in the community. But these are fewer than one might think. Those are a lot of plates to keep spinning all at the same time. And they must spin impeccably even though the spinning of the plates is not the organization's major job: healing the sick, singing the music, feeding the hungry or listening to the troubled is the work at hand.

What seems to keep a great number of non-profits from spinning these community plates is simple resentment. "Why do we have to take precious energy away from our work to go beg for money?... If only we could get some good media coverage the money would flow in here... Who would want to serve on this loser board?... I don't have **time** to thank people..." I have heard every one of those sentiments expressed over and over by harried and frustrated non-profit managers.

This book is meant to open a dialogue about the role community plays in all non-profits. It will explore all of the "shoulds" and "I can'ts". Non-profit organizations must think about their image in their communities and how that image got established. What do you want the community to think of you? What do you want them to do for and with you? How would community involvement change your organization?

This book will also illuminate for people in the community how you can grow personally and professionally by involving yourselves in non-profit organizations. Often the work you do every day is somewhat less than fulfilling or gratifying. You put in your time, take home your pay, and wonder what else there is. Or perhaps you have skills that you're not using to benefit humankind. You may have worked a full and rewarding career and are ready to retire, but not from the human race. If you fit into any of these categories, there is a non-profit organization that needs you. And it's not just money that's needed. Without your active participation, non-profit organizations are closed circles, spinning in their own small universe, talking only to themselves and wondering what's going wrong.

The secret ingredient for thousands of non-profit organizations is community involvement. It means giving up power to outside people, learning to ask for what **they** need and to say thank you, but it is the difference between mere survival and excellence.

This book is about community/non-profit partnership in an exciting project called fundraising: the community that has a need and the non-profit that exists to meet that need working together for the common community good.

My style of fundraising is blue collar, no apologies. I graduated from the school of Hard Knocks: learning how to raise money by trial and error (mostly error, it felt at the time). I started asking for large individual gifts by asking prospects to meet with me to talk about their "support". Support, it turned out, was a hearty pat on the back and the assurance that I was "doing a good job". Support's great. What I really wanted was money. Once I understood that myself, I worked out my approach. It turned out to be incredibly simple: I approach asking for money, whether it's for a special event, through the mail, over the phone, or in person, exactly the same way I approach someone I'd like to get to know. It's putting my personal best foot forward. Listening. Common sense and common decency. It's thank-you notes and table manners. It's inspiration more than evaluation, instinct over second thought. It's making friends--not just for my organization but for me and the person I'm approaching.

And as in all blue collar labor, it's part heart and a whole lot of sweat equity. For me, fundraising is worrying: will it work? Will anyone give? What did I forget? Late night dementia. Research and rewrites. More worry.

There are two reasons why I stay in fundraising. One is the feeling I get when I get the gift. It's quite a rush to work hard at creating a fundraising strategy that winds up making everyone feel good (win-win-win-win...) and brings in the money. Being carried around a boardroom by twenty happy non-profit folks is my idea of a good time. The other reason I stay in this field is because of the people I get to work with: Bob Bornhoeft, Betsy Richardson, Frank Brennan and Tracy Gary. Volunteers who come to fundraising with love, joy and humor. I would ride on the shoulders of my proven team off the face of a cliff, and fly every time.

What I have to share in these pages will save you some of the less glorious Seat-of-the-Pants experiences that I have stored up over the years. But this is not really a How-To book. You will find some How-To advice in these pages, but that is secondary. The purpose of this book is to adjust your attitude about fundraising, non-profits and community partnership. This book explains how fundraising can be more than money. This book challenges you to look through the money to the people and opportunities within the campaigns and events. Just behind the money is the community, and they have needs that you can meet. It is in the coming together to meet their needs and your needs that the heart of fundraising is revealed.

I would like to thank my patient, talented and gentle editor, Beverly Galley, for contributing to the text, production and style of this book. Thanks to Flo Green, my fundraising teacher, who gave me the opportunity to discover my love of teaching. Thanks to Kris Rebillot, Dianna Good, Susi Scribner, Debra Kent Friedland, Richard Raznikov, Michael Durphy, and Kim Klein for adding their wisdom to this production. And thank you, Cathy Tennant, for your hours at the computer and your unflagging faith in this project.

Part I
Cause and Community

CHAPTER ONE
Non-Profits and the Community

Why Non-profits?

Non-profit organizations exist to meet a need or solve a problem that exists outside of them. When St. Vincent de Paul Society opens a soup kitchen, the problem they are addressing is not St. Vincent's problem. The hungry are everyone's problem. If that soup kitchen did not exist, someone would have to start one. If no one came forward, those hungry people would be on our doorsteps asking for food. And if we did not feed them, they would die there and we would still be faced with solving the problems of suffering and death. St. Vincent de Paul Society acts in the name of all society to solve our common problem of how to feed the hungry.

In the non-profit world, need comes first. The non-profit organization exists to respond to a need or solve a problem. There is no incentive to stimulate need. For many life-and-death organizations we wish the need would go away: AIDS

Non-profits act in the name of all society to solve our common problems.

Need comes first.

cured, the homeless sheltered, the cycle of battering women and children stopped. Even in the arts, stimulating need does not mean artificially stimulating the market so that people "hunger" for your productions. It may mean having to educate the public about your particular brand of art or dance or music. But the "need" for the arts exists outside of the art organizations. Since it is art that translates civilization from one generation to the next, "art" is a quality of life need that cannot be disputed.

From human need flow services and programs. Once the need is identified by the non-profit, the strategy to meet that need is expressed by the development of a program. If the need you are addressing is child care, how do you propose solving the problem? Offering day care is one solution. But there are other parts to the problem. Like Project Care in San Rafael, California, you could meet the need by referring parents to low cost programs, helping to monitor the quality of day care in your community, and even running a revolving car seat loaner program. Or, like the Child Assault Prevention Project in Oakland, you could educate youngsters about what kind of touching is appropriate while they are in day care settings.

Services and programs flow from that need.

"Why do we exist?" But isn't this the simplest of questions? No. In fact, it is the biggest of stumbling blocks. Answer this question for yourself. Suppose you are the Gay and Lesbian Community Services Center. Why do you exist? Of course, "To help." To help whom? The answer to that question cannot be, "Everyone." You're just one organization in Los Angeles. "To help gay men and lesbians. And straight people who don't

What is your dream? The answer cannot be, "To help everyone."

understand us." Then the question must be, "Help them do what? What needs can you meet?" The answer to that question is often a shopping list of services, but that list does not answer the why of it. Why have a clinic? an employment program? a youth group? Why do advocacy? What do you want to accomplish? What is your dream? And how much of that dream can you carry out?

Non-profit organizations have a difficult time focusing vision on what they can accomplish because most of the work is a bandaid on a very large wound. Start with the knowledge that bandaging your part of the hurt is important. So long as you stay focused on the job of bandaging, you see clearly that your particular bandage is the absolute best it can be.

...a bandaid on a very large wound

Once your organization has decided what you will offer to the community to get at the community's need, you are ready for the business plan. This part is sometimes overlooked by zealous and stressed non-profits. What will happen for what people at what cost? Where will the money come from? How do you want to grow over the coming years? Who do you need to help you? Until your business plan is in place, your organization is not ready to fundraise.

Until your business plan is in place, you are not ready to fundraise.

The Non-Profit as a Business

"Business" may be the most misunderstood word in the non-profit vocabulary (with "marketing" a close second). Most people who choose the non-profit sector as their focus for a career do so to find an alternative to the business world where you make money, hustle customers, and do work that benefits the world not at all. Non-profit work has generally lower pay and longer hours, but it is perceived as being full of passion and purpose. Where does a business plan fit into an organization that is engrossed in saving the world?

In the for-profit world, a business plan is a blueprint for production and sales. A good manager will sit down and figure out how many widgets can be produced, how much each one costs to produce, how much she or he can sell them for, and who the potential market is. Services provided by non-profits are harder to quantify and cost out than are widgets. Community theaters often have a very difficult time figuring out how much it costs to produce a play. Of course they buy wood, paint, fabric for costumes, and they pay the bookkeeper and the general manager. But the hidden costs are difficult to trace without diligent effort because the Board President brings the doughnuts to rehearsals, the volunteers bring their own paint brushes and use their own sewing machines, "comp" tickets are available but it is not known if they are used, media contact is made by volunteers using their own telephones, and so on. An added problem with allowing hidden costs to stay hidden is that the Board President feels that she is "giving plenty" to the organization because of her bakery bills, and the other volunteers who are quietly paying out-of-pocket production expenses feel the same. When it comes time to ask for donations to pay for the up-front expenses, fundraising falls flat.

Where does a business plan fit?

The president brings the doughnuts...

...and feels she is "giving plenty" when she pays the bakery bill.

20

Having a Business Plan for a non-profit organization means knowing what your services cost to perform, including staff time, materials used, and a portion of the rent, utilities and overhead costs like accounting and supervising services. It is essential that you know exactly what it costs to see each client, produce each concert, or cook each meal so that you can charge an appropriate amount and then go to funding sources to make up the difference. While the general plea for "Help!" and having a fundraising goal of "as much as we can" has worked in the past, donors are getting more sophisticated and want to see that you're watching the balance sheet as well as the program.

Donors are getting more sophisticated.

Looking to the Future

Having a Business Plan also means taking the time to figure out where you are going and how you will get there. The Cancer Support Community is a new non-profit organization based in San Francisco. It began when two women met in the hospital and agreed that they were not getting the kinds of information they wanted and needed about cancer. The "heart" of the program is enabling a community of people who are struggling with cancer to offer loving support and encouragement to each other, along with providing reliable information.

...where you are going and how you will get there

When these two women were first asked, "How many people will you serve?" the answer was, "Everyone who needs us." So they began by answering every call for help at any hour of the day or night. They rushed to peoples' bedsides, they ran groups out of their living rooms, they took more and more referrals from hospitals and doctors - - all free of charge. And it became a dead end project: without money the two women could not feed themselves, let alone help the organization to prosper. So they made time to do fundraising. When they were asked, "How much do you need to raise?" they responded, "As much as we can." The problem with that goal is that it is unreachable. Try as you might, you will never raise as much as you can. There are always more grants to write, more potential donors to see, more corporations to approach.

In addition to knowing your costs, it is important to think about what the future holds for you. To really address the problem or meet the need, it is essential to know what the need will look like in five years, or ten years, and how strong you will need to be to address that need.

Let me say here that finding the time to plan is always a struggle. I've never seen an organization with time on their hands, looking for a way to fill it. But good, realistic planning is the most important gift you can give your organization. In their planning, the Cancer Support Community looked at how big the problem of cancer is in the Bay Area and how much it was likely to grow in the coming years. They determined what they would, and would not, provide to people with cancer. They decided how quickly their staff would grow to meet that need. They systematized referrals so that getting back to the referring physician would be easier, and the doctors developed more trust in their professionalism. Since they determined that all

Try as you might, you will never raise as much as you can.

Good, realistic planning is the most important gift you can give your organization.

services are free and will remain that way, they know that all costs must be covered by fundraising. With that much dependence on fundraising, they had to build in a staff position to see to the raising of money.

Still not convinced that you need to plan?

California NOW (National Organization for Women) at one time had no provision for planning. That thrust them into a mode of reaction instead of action, and they found themselves perched, gripping the edge of the precipice, waiting for the enemy to make a move. It is very difficult to raise money from people when your main argument is, "Look what they're doing now!" While the "Chicken Little" school of fundraising does draw in people who live in constant fear of the sky really falling, eventually, when the sky continues pale blue with occasional low clouds, the crisis pitch stops working. Also for NOW, staying poised to react meant that they were not out in front leading. If you are responding to the political climate, you are not helping to set and regulate it.

...the "Chicken Little" school of fundraising

The budgeting of time and energy was also of great concern to NOW. They could not set aside the important lobbying and fundraising work to create some visionary plan for the future. But they could not afford not to. NOW decided to bite the bullet and do it all, and it worked for them. In addition to their nine-to-five jobs, chapter activists did their political work **and** focused considerable energy on leadership development for the organization for an entire year.

You're Worthy of Support!

The notion of being different from "business" because your organization helps its fellow human beings often gets in the way of looking at yourselves with a keen business eye. We do good works. We pay ourselves subsistence wages. Why doesn't the world recognize this and throw money at us? This is called the Charity Mentality.

I did extensive work with a fairly large non-profit that runs shelters for the homeless. They believe that it is their duty to care for these people. From the Board down to the Shelter workers, each one knows that fundraising is important. Yet they refuse to even listen to a discussion about building an endowment to take care of the programs. With their donor demographics showing a population well into their sixties and very wealthy, deferred giving would be a natural approach. It would allow donors to provide for the shelters through wills and bequests. But these very well-meaning non-profit folks believe that it is their duty to take every cent they get and spend it on the homeless, even if it means a hand-to-mouth existence for the organization and added stress for all concerned about where the money will come from next year or next month. That is the Charity Mentality. The ironic part is that the Board has its share of business people who would not consider running **their** businesses so close to the bone.

Putting "Charity" or "Non-profit" at one pole and "Business" or "For-profit" at the opposite pole has gotten untold numbers of

The Charity Mentality

non-profit managers in deep trouble. The Shelter organization above has well over a $2 million annual budget. But what if one of their buildings collapses in the next earthquake? What if a funding source changes priorities? What if...? Without the buffer of even a savings account, the organization risks having to lay off people with no notice, closing shelters (leaving the very souls they are trying to help as bad off as the day they found them), and ultimately having to close the agency. While this is an extreme example, it is a common practice for non-profits to operate on a deficit, with "nest eggs" being extremely rare. Calamity is always just around the corner. I maintain that if a non-profit is a flash in the pan, or succumbs to preventable calamity, leaving the audience or clients without services, it has indeed provided no real service to the community after all.

An ugly outgrowth of all this, the Tin Cup Mentality, happens when the Charity Mentality collides with fundraising. This distorted view of fundraising arises partly from misdirected altruism and partly from a dead-in-the-water fear of asking for money.

The Tin Cup mentality takes a fundraising goal and reduces it to nickels and dimes. "We have to raise $20,000!" your group laments. A Tin Cup strategy would be a membership drive aimed at finding 1000 to give you $20 each. While those 1000 people are absolutely vital to your organization, I guarantee you that in that pool are 100 who would give you $200 each, requiring ten times the research energy but one-hundredth of the organizing and asking time. Pushing it even further, I also

If a non-profit succumbs to preventable calamity, it has provided no real service to the community after all.

guarantee you that, if you spent perhaps twice again the research energy, you could identify four people who would give you $5000 each.

When I work with grassroots groups on fundraising and we approach this formula, I always get resistance. "NO!" they ex___m. "No one would give us large gifts! We're just little X__ Agency!" If you are feeling this reluctance, know, first, that the discomfort you're experiencing is your own discomfort, not that of the donor. And second, keep reading... because this book was written for you.

Why Do We Have to Do Money?

One of the problems inherent in trying to climb out of second class status, personified by the Tin Cup Mentality, is the fear that it just might be true. Maybe we **can't** make it in the world of big donors, in corporate boardrooms, in society. Maybe we **are** dreamers, bleeding heart liberals, wimps. Maybe our work just **isn't** important enough. It is, after all, just one little organization facing a big, cruel world. And somehow, money taints our altruism. One organization I worked with had created the internal mantra, "It's exceedingly embarrassing to have to ask for money." Every Board member could recite that perfectly, and did so often.

One hot-bed of this form of self-hypnosis is the art world. Picture the artist, struggling to pay his or her rent, living in a

The Tin Cup Mentality

The discomfort you are feeling is your own.

How To Lose Donors Like Crazy

Tip #1: *Remember that no one really wants to give to you, so before you approach them, say "no" for them. Saves time.*

world of colors and shapes. Ask this person how well their business is going and you will see a frail hand lifted to a pale forehead..."I do art. I don't do money." It has become acceptable for "true" artists to retreat in confusion when money is mentioned, as though those people do not have to eat or pay for their lodging. I received a call just this morning from a young man who was hoping to find a student to run a company. The company is made up of professional musicians who like to play chamber music together now and then. They do music. They wanted to find someone to volunteer to do business... to write a grant "or something" to pay for his own salary and to arrange everything about the concerts: mailings, programs, halls, etc. The young man mentioned that they have a few volunteers who come in and sell refreshments at intermissions, and I suggested that several of those volunteers might be willing to share these tasks. "But that would take so much time! I could never ask them to do that." This organization will stay stuck, violas to the wall, until they decide that in order to do music they also must do business.

Environmentalists do it too: "I'll lead the groups, but someone else must sell the tickets." Women's groups do it: "We've been oppressd by money so long, let's not talk about it." It cuts across all lines in non-profit work. WHY DO WE HAVE TO DO MONEY?!

We "have to do money" for the same reason we "have to" provide child care, health care, and art: the need is there and we must step forward to meet that need.

"I do art. I don't do money."

27

How to Conduct a Bake Sale

A Bake Sale is an event where anyone with an oven can bake you anything sweet. You sell this to anyone who will buy it for as much money as you can get. Why do it? Because everybody can do it, it is a familiar activity, you have lots of well-meaning volunteers who want to do it, and nobody is embarrassed. Because it seems so much easier to bake, package and sell cookies than to ask someone to write a check.

Start with: How much money do you need to raise this year to make your organization viable?

So, you need $36,000. Let's figure it out. There are 52 Saturdays per year. If you can get $.50 per cookie, you will need:

* 72,000 cookies
* 18 people to bake 4000 cookies each
* 2172 volunteer hours per year (36 volunteer hours per Saturday, with two people per site per six-hour shift) to sell them
* 1576 cookies per Saturday sold at 3 sites (500+ cookies per site)
* $13 gross raised per volunteer hour (including the bakers)

This gross fundraising figure presumes that the volunteer bakers and sellers are picking up the costs of:

chocolate chips	flour
walnuts	butter
plastic wrap	labels
signs	gasoline
baby sitters	etc.

The Way to Start: Go to your next Board meeting and say, "I've got a great idea. Let's do a Bake Sale!"

You cannot do this unless:
* Your community has passed through, or not yet reached, the health food phase; and

* Your cookies and your sales force are better than the Girl Scouts'; and

* You have at least 200 volunteers willing to give up weekends, including major holidays and during Little League season.

Details to consider:
  Gloves in the winter
  Mosquito netting in the summer
  Enough quarters to make change
  Packaging the cookies so they look irresistible
  Sunscreen
  Comfortable folding chairs
  Marking pens that don't run in the rain

If you must do a Bake Sale, remember that you might make more money if you go to where the people are: Farmers Market, the 4th of July County Fair, the Mall, etc. To be fair, Camp Fire and the Girl Scouts make tons of money on candy and cookie sales, but they don't bake them or package them, and they have professional marketing help on a nationwide basis. They also do their sales during a very limited time span. So do Bake Sales if you must, but please do not expect to make very much money.

At this point your Board has two options:

1) Bake 72,000 cookies and borrow lots of card tables and spend three out of every five weekends for the next year in front of Safeway; OR (!)

2) Your eighteen Board members can raise $2000 each over the next year, including their own gift.

Point?

If Bake Sales mark your fundraising comfort level right now, start immediately to raise it.

Beyond the Tin Cup Mentality

You read a lot about how Americans are the most generous people in the world, but please do not swallow that whole. We are a rich nation and many people, rich and poor, understand the importance of the work being done by the non-profit sector. But stop for a minute and take a look at the attitude Americans have toward fundraising and the people who make a living doing it. They use words like "getting hit up", they brag about hanging up on telephone solicitations and throwing out "junk mail" without opening it. I once traveled across the country in an airplane sitting next to a man who bragged both about his extensive wealth and about the fact that he's never given away a dime.

The really bad news about all of this is that non-profit people buy right into it. Look in your heart and answer this question: Do you believe that fundraising is something like begging? Most of the people who come to my fundraising seminars do. And they are the people who are out there trying to raise money! No one wants to be a beggar. In begging one person asks another person to do something and get nothing in return, except perhaps rid of the beggar.

Fundraising is very different. Fundraising starts with the realization that what you are raising money **for** is something of value. Whether it's a magnificent vocal chorus, an essential low cost dental clinic, or a consumer rights group for seniors, think about what it is about your organization that is so wonderful.

No one wants to be a beggar.

That certain something is something of value. But that something of value cannot happen, cannot perform, serve and meet a need, without something else of value, which is money. It is very important to know that the something of value which is your great program and the something of value which is the money that makes it happen are **equal.** Not only are they equal, but you cannot separate them, because without the money the program goes away or is diminished. So, going out into the community, asking people for money, is in fact inviting them to be your partner in making something of value happen. They cannot be on the front line serving food to the hungry or painting scenery or driving children to the opera. They are off doing what they do to make a living. But **do not presume** that they do not care about the work you are doing. By inviting them to write a check and make the program happen, you are giving them an **opportunity** to feel as good about the program as you do. You are bringing the community in to take part in the good work. By writing a check to make your organization happen, your community gains the opportunity to feel some **ownership** in a rewarding activity. In fact, that rewarding activity is designed specifically to meet a community need or solve a community problem.

We are back to the understanding that from need flows program, and then fundraising happens. The need is the need of the community, whether it is for regional theater, crime prevention or day care. Your non-profit exists to meet that need. Good fundraising means much more than just money. It is a program designed to give the ownership back where it

Something of Value.

They cannot be on the front line... but do not presume that they don't care.

From need flows program, and then fundraising happens.

31

belongs: to the community. The need that is being met is theirs. By writing a check, they are participating in the solution.

Relating to the Corporate Sector

OF COURSE non-profit organizations are businesses. As a matter of fact, at this moment they make up more than 8% of the gross national product. They buy computers, housing, vans and cars, paper, and untold numbers of post-it-notes. They employ people. They pay rent. And a fact that often comes as news to many non-profits is that "non-profit" does not mean **no** profit. It means that no one person or group of people may profit. If you are a non-profit it is not necessary to finish the year with red ink. As a matter of fact, the Girl Scouts require that every Council have one year's operating budget in the bank. That's good business sense.

But still the non-profit sector shies away from thinking of itself in business terms. And this prejudice rears its ugly head most vividly when the non-profit organization approaches a corporation for volunteers, in-kind donations or money. It usually does not feel like one business going to another business to solicit cooperation. It feels more like going, hat in hand, to "the establishment".

In fundraising trainings, I often ask groups of non-profit executives, "What words come to mind when I say

The Girl Scouts require that every Council have one year's operating budget in the bank. That's just good business sense.

'corporations'?" While the standard impressions (profit, glass towers, board rooms) surface, I also consistently hear "pigs", "arrogant", "cheap", "old boy network", etc. This is not a good attitude to have when you are going to ask someone to work with you. Tom Boyd, a fundraising consultant in New York City, was formerly a Corporate Giving Officer. He reports that Giving Officers have a recurring nightmare. They sit down at a desk stacked high with funding requests. Up from the pile comes a hand, grabbing them by front of the shirt, and a voice booms out: "Okay, pig ... Give!" (They **know** what you're thinking!)

"Okay, pig . . . Give!"

Obviously, for-profit business is perceived as being "where the money is." In the early 1980's, as President Reagan began slashing non-profit organizations from the national budget and agenda, he called for corporations to take up the slack. Non-profits were hopeful. On some levels it made sense: The money's there, and that sector has been notoriously cheap in sharing the wealth. Why **not** have them step in and give?

Well, first there's the small matter of the economy and how capitalism works. For-profit businesses do not exist to give away money. If one were foolish enough to do that, pretty soon their employees would be in St. Vincent de Paul's soup line. They exist to make money and they have to answer to their stockholders, so most giving programs are very small. In order to gain more insight into why and how corporations flourish, and certainly to gain more knowledge of how your non-profit can approach the business at hand, I recommend

Their employees would soon be in St. Vincent de Paul's soup line.

Tom Peters' *In Search of Excellence.*

Now, take a step back and think about the way the corporate sector views the non-profit world. How do you think a roomful of corporate executives would respond if I asked, "What do you think of when I say 'non-profit' worker?" They might say: Birkenstocks and bleeding hearts, sloppy managers, can't make it in the corporate world, dreamers... The myth of who they are has its own corresponding myth of who we are. And who gets to take responsibility for breaking down the walls of the myth? We do, of course.

So, how can non-profits begin to face the planning and fundraising work they have to do? First, accept responsibility for changing how non-profits are perceived in the business community as well as the community-at-large.

   Step one: Start running your organization as though it were a business. That means benefit packages for employees, budget and program planning, annual reports to the community, the whole works.

   Step two: Find creative ways to expose your organization to the community as a business. One good way is to join the Chamber of Commerce, which usually has non-profit rates for membership. Then you get to stand up at meetings and introduce yourself and your organization. Business leaders get to see that you are not some strange holdover from 1965 but business-like and personable. Another good way to project

Who gets the responsibiliy for breaking down the myths? We do, of course.

...benefit packages, budget and program planning, annual reports, the whole works

34

your business face to the world is to have representatives of your organization serve on civic ad hoc committees: planning parades, organizing downtown clean-ups or Spring art contests, etc. Image is very important here. Millions of us watched an episode of *60 Minutes* featuring a very controversial environmental group. Everyone featured looked like a caricature: ratty jeans, messy hair. One guy played the guitar and sang a folk song about their work. Like, wow! I know that there were folks watching who would send money, join their group, and support them in untold numbers of ways — and I believe in their work. But their image stops me. While they look perfectly capable of chaining themselves to trees and singing, I do not for one minute believe in their ability to communicate with corporate America about the alternatives to raping our planet. When one group of people wants the cooperation of another group of people, it is the first group's responsibility to persuade the second group using words they understand. Save hitting them over the head with 2 x 4's for the last resort.

Step three: Involve other business people in the governing of your organization. I do not advocate putting together an all-business or an all-anything Board. The best Boards are diverse and rich in their different experiences. But I also worry that non-profits are allowing their fear of corporate people to get in the way of tapping the rich resources of expertise and contacts that exist in the for-profit sector. They're part of the community, too. In addition to utilizing business people on your Boards, consider inviting them to help develop budgets, plan

They're part of the community, too.

35

fundraising campaigns, audit your books or any other number of ad hoc activities. I have found it helpful to "test" future Board members by having them volunteer for specific tasks and see how they follow through.

Taking down the walls is **your** job. The sooner you get to it, the sooner you'll begin uniting your community.

CHAPTER TWO
Finding Your Community

Who Do You Serve?

That's a fairly straightforward question. If you are a low cost dental clinic, you serve low income people who need dental care. But who else do you serve? In fact, you serve the dentists in town who do not accept welfare patients, you serve the volunteers who come in to help with third party billing, you serve the staff who rely on you for timely paychecks, and you serve the Board who proudly govern your organization. If you are fuzzy about who you really serve, at your next staff and/or Board meeting brainstorm a list: other than clients/audience, whose lives are affected because you exist? Your list will probably include businesses, schools, nursing homes, police, teachers, paper suppliers, van mechanics and all kinds of folks who benefit from your work.

Who Needs the Arts?

Picture a ballet dancer with a dream of what ballet should be. He assembles the most talented students he can find, rents a wonderful inexpensive performance space, gets a friend to print up a flyer, and puts on a show. Twenty-seven people attend. Whose needs are being met? The obvious answer is that the twenty-seven people, the dancers and perhaps the folks making money on the hall and the flyer are all getting some of their needs met. If twenty-six people attend the next performance, is

the need shrinking? If twenty-eight show up, is it growing?
Who is art for? Performers and artists? The critics who make a
living off it? The corporations that sponsor it? The audience
that attends the performances? The Board of the non-profit
sponsoring organization?

Arts organizations have perpetually focused on the audience as
the primary group of people whose needs must be met. The San
Francisco Ballet produced a major fundraising effort in 1987 to
totally revamp their Nutcracker sets and costumes. They were
not doing that to attract new audience, because new audience
would not have known that the sets were previously used.
They were doing it to rekindle interest in the Nutcracker from
traditional attendees. But spending so much time, money and
energy holding on to your ongoing audience has its
disadvantages.

First there is the problem of the "graying" of the audience. This
means that people who attend live performances or go to
museums tend to be older, and younger people are not taking
their place. Our society has suffered through years of
misguided belt-tightening that included removing "fluff" from
our fiscally strapped schools. Unfortunately, we've discovered
that you cannot educate half a brain: without music, math has
little purpose. We are now a society full of young people who
think "enrichment" is achieved through a second job, and who
leave experiencing art to their elders. Older people tend to have
money to spend on live performances, and so the ticket prices
keep rising — which shuts out younger **and** older low-income

Who is art for?

38

folks. If the organization's focus is on keeping the audience happy, they must face the sad fact that the audience is getting older and dying. Then they must answer the difficult question: whose job is it to educate young people and encourage them to appreciate the arts? And whose job is it to draw in curious but bewildered, undereducated young adults?

Ultimately this problem will fall on the shoulders of the empty museums and concert halls. It is in everyone's best interest to challenge the arts to replace their vision with a broader one, to look way beyond "audience" to the greater "community". If "audience" as a prospect pool is the size of New Jersey, "community" as a prospect pool is the size of Asia. If an arts organization has tax-exempt status, their 501(c)(3), they do not exist just to give their art to the select few who show up for performances or gallery shows. Their tax-exempt status means that they have a responsibility to the community in which they live.

Arts organizations, like all other non-profits, affect the community around them, whether or not those community people ever walk through their doors. The low cost clinic affects the entire community because it takes care of people who cannot afford health care, people whose ill health would eventually impact others in the community. In the same way, the local artists' collective is keeping talented people from abandoning their art, keeping local art productive and alive. This vitalizes an entire community whether the residents make, buy or even appreciate art. It raises the quality of the life of the community.

If "audience" as a prospect pool is the size of New Jersey, "community" as a prospect pool is the size of Asia.

But traditionally, when that collective runs out of money to put on the classes for artists or mount a new show, they are at a loss for who to turn to. The people who buy their art pay for the product they're getting, "So why should they give?" The artists have no money. Perhaps a foundation would fund them. But why should a foundation care any more or less than their neighbors might? In fact, the usual scenario is that the neighbors have never been invited to see the collective's works, never invited to attend a class, because the artists think they would not be interested. The neighbors think they're not welcome or, at best, have no idea what the collective does.

The demise of the Oakland Symphony is an excellent case in point. They were a top quality orchestra, had monied and influential people on their Board, and had a magnificent concert hall in which to showcase their work. Unfortunately, the Board made some very bad financial decisions that threw them into deep debt, and their turn-over of conductors and unsure approach to the next season sped the process. The entire process is studied and analyzed in an excellent report commissioned by the Symphony's funders after the fact so that other orchestras would not follow in their footsteps. But the real lesson to be learned from this autopsy, I believe, has more to do with community relations than with bookkeeping and personnel. Oakland is one of the most dynamic, and depressed, communities of the Bay Area. While drug dealing is murderously prevalent, the concerted efforts of neighborhoods, churches and community activists to eradicate the problem are very exciting. There are model youth programs, comprehensive day care programs, and urban redevelopment projects that are bringing new hope and vitality to Oakland. The "art" jewels in this crown were the Symphony and their exquisitely restored art deco Paramount Theater. The problem, according to the autopsy, was that the orchestra's focus was not on their community but on competing with the San Francisco Symphony, trying to attract audience away from the city and to Oakland. They wanted to be the premier Symphony in the Bay Area.

In the course of the autopsy, the interviewers discovered that Board members were still bemoaning the fact that they were never able to get their biggest donor/Board member to attend the performances. They were focused on him as "audience". He didn't care for that kind of music, but was focused beyond the music to community-building. He saw beyond the song. Looking at the Symphony as a building block for Oakland, through the Symphony he was investing in community. That is an entirely different way to look at the work all non-profits do in their communities, and every bit as valid. What a tremendous opportunity they missed! They could have been partners in the rebirth of Oakland. With a different vision, they could have taken their place as citizens of the new Oakland, bringing symphony music to people and places that would use it as a food to make a community grow.

A Word about Free Social Welfare Programs

In social service programs "partnership" usually feels like marriage, with the needy and their needs continually under your nose, and "community" usually means the numbers of people demanding your services.

Part of the community you are addressing is certainly your clients. But the "community" I am speaking of is much bigger than that. Working in the social services means that you must be able to focus on what is right in front of you – your clients. But you must be able to stand back and look out to the larger "community" beyond them. So, in the search for partnership, begin by asking yourself: Do you provide free services to the indigent? Are your health care services, your family planning clinics, your hot lunches and used clothes all given free of charge? If so, I ask you to stop and think about the message you are giving to your clients and to your donors and the community.

First, think about the notion that giving people the opportunity to write a check and become your partner is the real heart and soul of fundraising. You are saying to people with money, "You can be our partners in helping poor people to eat and receive health care, and you can take pride and great joy in making this important program happen."

Giving people the opportunity to write a check and become your partner is the heart and soul of fundraising.

Do you buy that? Is that the kind of relationship you would like to have with your donors? If so, you are on the right fundraising track.

Now think about what you are saying to your clients when you give them a free service but ask for nothing in return. You are saying, "You poor people can get this service but you cannot be a part of making this organization happen for yourself and others. You may only receive the service. You are not our partners, just the recipients of our charity."

In the long run, are you doing a real service to the people you serve? Or are you building dependence and helping to shatter their self-esteem? I fully understand that homeless people cannot pay for the cots they occupy or the soup they gratefully drink. I am not even really talking about money here. The few dollars or even cents are not the issue. The issue is partnership.

The tragedy of homelessness is not just the problem of people out on the streets. It's the problem of everyone who pays taxes expecting Americans to be taken care of at least minimally. It's the problem of businesses who find the homeless begging/sleeping/living at their doorsteps every day. It's also the problem of the police, and of the hospitals who take care of the homeless when they are cold and sick. It's the problem of caring people who look into the eyes of the homeless and know that something must be done. It's the problem of our children who will inherit the problem, still unsolved. But if all of us who enjoy a roof over our heads banded together to solve the problem of homelessness without including the homeless, we would be in serious trouble because 1) we do not know what it's really like out there–what are the actual needs; 2) we will fail until we learn that many of the homeless are as capable as

"You are not our partners, just the recipients of our charity."

43

we are of taking care of themselves, but circumstances have robbed them of the opportunity; and 3) while many of the homeless need taking care of, most just need someone to care.

Imagine what would happen if the homeless banded together without **us** to solve **our** problems! Same problem, inside out.

The example of the homeless situation is extreme, but it carries forward. The issue is the same for people in any dire straits: leaving them out of the solution is a big mistake. Giving them free services and goods continues the cycle of the poor as needy victims instead of human beings who can help end suffering.

If you ask community people to write checks to provide services to the poor, what can you ask the poor to do? A hot meal is worth something to the person eating it. It might be worth 15 minutes cleaning up. Or perhaps 20 minutes stuffing envelopes. Let's take the example further. What about the non-abled body? What about the person with AIDS who is receiving three meals a day from a non-profit program? What are those meals worth? Perhaps he could make a phone call to a Foundation thanking them for their gift. Or maybe he could give the organization the names of 20 friends to ask for money, and allow his name to be used in the letter. He might even have the strength to appear in a video about the services of the organization.

Social service organizations have often stayed away from such strategies because of **their own** discomfort in asking clients to give back for the services they receive. Some perhaps feel that it

The issue is the same for people in any dire straits: leaving them out of the solution is a big mistake.

44

is too much trouble to develop the guidelines and monitor them. But I want social service organizations to think about the self-esteem issue. Imagine yourself in a position where, for whatever reason, you cannot take care of yourself and must be cared for by strangers.

The Marin Home Care services in Marin County, California, serves people in their homes who are elderly and sick, recovering from an illness, or suffering a chronic disabling illness. They provide physical and occupational therapy and nursing assistance. In 1989 they participated in "The Human Race". They sent a letter to their clients, the majority of whom are on welfare, asking them to pledge money to support the marathon effort of their "favorite therapist". One elderly woman I know who lives on a little more than $400 per month not only sent a check for $25, but included a thank-you note for being asked. She was proud of being able to honor someone who had helped her so much.

It is interesting that, while social services for the poor strive to keep people alive, they often overlook human dignity. Our own discomfort with asking for money, and seeing peoples' lack of it, often gets in the way of stepping up and inviting folks to chip in and make a difference, and feel good about themselves. Please do not overlook your clients as you build your case for partnership.

One elderly woman not only sent a check, but included a thank-you note for being asked.

Beyond The Board: Inviting Community Input

Looking out into the community for partnership will surely mean finding some good-hearted volunteers who want to help you in your quest. You know that you need fundraising, and you and your volunteers reach for the handiest way to structure that activity. The model for creating a volunteer fundraising structure is fairly standard: get three or four Board members to be on the fundraising committee and charge them with raising the dollars you need.

There are several flaws in this model. First, I have rarely seen a "fundraising committee" of the Board who were 100% electrified about their task. They are usually a mix of people who are well-intentioned, eager for the organization to succeed, and reluctant to ask for money. Secondly, they are hardly ever trained. Somehow organizations expect THE BOARD (them!) to figure it out. And with a set-up like this, when the organization runs out of money, the Board looks to the committee and wonders, not benignly, "What is THE FUNDRAISING COMMITTEE doing?"

But the tragic flaw is that when your Board governs, and your Board designs and executes the fundraising in the community, the community comes to perceive your organization as a closed circle. New blood comes to your fundraising only when new people come to your Board and they somehow make their way onto your fundraising committee.

. . . the Board wonders, not benignly, "What is THE FUNDRAISING COMMITTEE doing?"

"New blood" is an important concept to non-profit organizations. The down side of the concept of constantly looking for new blood is that the task never ends. Recruitment of people **with** energy takes a tremendous amount **of** it. Most non-profits back off from this task and cling instead to the concept of getting the perfect mix of Board members and keeping them forever. There are at least a half-dozen problems with this:

❖ Old age and death.

❖ Burn-out before old age and death.

❖ Falling into a routine meeting structure where not only are issues predictable, but everyone in the room knows what everyone else in the room will say in their closing arguments.

❖ It's hard to find new donors when your askers never change.

❖ Your organization becomes identified with a particular "circle" of people and it becomes difficult to talk about your issues or needs in the community.

❖ Often cliques form and fight each other.

I worked with an agency that stuck to this model. Now and then a new Board member would join, but usually stayed on the periphery and never quite figured out where he or she belonged.

The old Board members, some of whom were founders, never left. They raised astonishing sums of money through major gifts and they gave a black tie dinner for nearly 1000 people every year. Sound good? They also scoffed at "little ticket" fundraising, including the organization's yearly Membership Drive that raised nearly $50,000 through $25 to $100 donations. Every year, the Board invited and cajoled their friends to come to the dinner, which hooked the event to their personalities and not to the organization—-jeopardizing the future of that fundraising activity. The year that I was in the fundraiser's seat, the Board decided to spend $50,000 on entertainment for the dinner. When that was added to the lavish hotel ballroom costs, wine on every table, extremely fancy invitations and ad books, the event grossed over $170,000 and netted a mere $25,000. When the community discovered these figures, there was a minor scandal. But these Board members were so powerful that they brushed off the publicity and congratulated themselves on throwing another great party. Sometimes it's okay to give a party just for your friends, but this Board had lost sight of the organization they served and its long-term need for a healthy donor base.

Another organization in Northern California that operates on this model has created for itself an interesting contradiction. The organization serves low-income physically handicapped people. Salaries are low, turnover high, and the staff fairly disgruntled. But the Board are all monied people. Most have signed on because this is where their friends are. They attend Board meetings and expect, and receive, lunch. They all know the same prospects and complain when asked to solicit them one more time. But they do a yearly mailing to these prospects, they run a very successful elite auction at a local estate attended by these same prospects, and they have started major gift

How To Lose Donors Like Crazy

Tip #5: *If the donor's link – a Board or staff person or a volunteer – leaves the organization, assume that the donor is no longer interested. Never invite them to anything again. Do this selectively so that some friends get invited and some friends do not.*

48

asking... of these same prospects. What will happen when these Board askers retire, or grow tired of the organization? What will happen when two or three of the key Board people leave and it's no longer a club? Would you guess that the donors and prospects will leave, too?

Do not lose the point here. It is good to have Board members and volunteers who solicit their friends and neighbors. It is bad if these new donors feel connected only to the asker and not to the organization. In order for this connecting to happen, it is not enough for the askers to deliver the bodies: they must turn them over to the organization to be cared for, cultivated, and helped to feel ownership. In the Northern California example above, the major gift askers on the Board will not tell the Executive Director nor any other staff who they are soliciting! They say that they are "protective" of their prospects. It is clear that the prospects, and eventually the donors, will be so well protected from the organization that they'll follow that asker anywhere, including on to the next non-profit he fancies.

Board, volunteer and donor development is about more than just finding them. It's really about connecting them to your organization, and giving them a chance to be heard and make a difference. Inviting community input means leaving room for non-Board volunteers and donors on your committees and in your fundraising activities. Moreover, I recommend that non-Board volunteers **chair** fundraising activities. The way this works is to identify community people who have good energy and contacts and express an interest in fundraising. Rather than

How To Lose Donors Like Crazy

Tip #15: *When writing to older donors, always use the smallest type your printer can find.*

It is not enough for the askers to deliver the bodies.

Connecting them to your organization, giving them a chance to be heard and to make a difference.

49

pouncing on them to join the Board (which in some instances will scare them away), invite them to help create your next special event. Put them on the food task force. Let them hustle restaurants and caterers and see how they do. If they do great, put them in charge of the food booth at the event: coordinating volunteers and replenishing food with the pressure on from the crowd. If they do great, next year they chair it. And the year after. The third year they are invited to join the Board. With this kind of system, you will be bringing on trained and proven Board members. And if you are constantly looking for good volunteers, you will gain a reputation as an organization that knows how to put volunteers to good work, and they will find you. And as you add new volunteers to your fundraising activities, you will add their circles of friends to your donor list.

How Foundations Fit

Donors! Volunteers! Boards! As organizations face the need to raise money, all of these systems seem overwhelming. "It takes so much time!" they lament. "I don't need a Board," they claim. "I know what we need....

"Let's just get a nice big grant and our worries will be over."

Getting a nice big grant is just what you **don't** want to do. Even if Foundations were in the business of providing the bulk of your funding, giving a Foundation that much power is the opposite of what you need.

You will gain a reputation as an organization that knows how to put volunteers to good work.

"I know what we need! We need...

50

Think of your organization as a giant slab of concrete. If you raise it up and provide only one source of support under it, it will wobble and fall. The best thing that can happen for your organization is that it have thousands of hands holding it up. If one or two leave, others will replace them, giving money every year, supporting your cause or program in the community, and making your organization very stable.

If a foundation wants to give you a large chunk of money and tell you how to run your program, consider this proposition very carefully. Remember that from **need** flows **program**, and then **fundraising** makes sense. Then the money is being raised to conduct a program that will meet a real need. If one funding source is dictating what the program should be in order for your organization to get the money, then you will have reversed this flow and the community's need is no longer the focus.

There are other dangers, too. A few years ago, a wealthy resident made a bequest, in the form of oil company stock, to the people of my county. In her will, she asked the San Francisco Foundation to use the stock proceeds to support the needy in Marin County through non-profits working in the areas of health, social welfare, the arts and religion. She happened to die during the oil crisis; virtually overnight the stock skyrocketed in value and the estate was worth several hundred million dollars. By law, the San Francisco Foundation was to distribute annually the interest — now

...a nice big grant!"

...thousands of hands

51

many millions of dollars— in Marin County. As you might guess, the San Francisco Foundation soon became the sole source of funding for many non-profits: other foundations declined to give in the county because of this huge trust, and many individuals living here felt that the trust would take care of all of the non-profits' needs. Some non-profits flourished. Others that were not favored by the Foundation died on the vine. Then, after a very ugly legal battle, the trust was transferred to a newly-created entity, the Marin Community Foundation. They surveyed the community, added their own issues and priorities, and somewhat changed the focus of giving. So we saw non-profits which had been feeling snug and confidant of continued giving literally go out of business. With only one source to go to, their options for alternative funding were nil.

Going to foundations for money makes sense if 1) you want to start up a new program; 2) you have a new project that you are itching to launch; or 3) you need technical assistance money to hire an expert to help you take the next big step. Once your organization is stable, your donor programs in place, and your program humming along, foundations are not all that interested in you and you are really beyond needing grants to get by. The important thing to remember is that foundation grants by themselves do not make you stable. They get you started and in many cases give you the energy, credibility and encouragement to go ahead and build a stable base. But if you want to give

If you want to give your organization what it needs to flourish, look to the community for money.

your organization the kind of base it needs to flourish, look to the community for money.

Where Do Corporations Belong In Your Strategy?

Corporations are part of the community, and the word "partnership" still works when considering how to work with this sector of donors. But when non-profits begin to think about working with corporate givers, one very large problem arises: Attitude. Part of the attitude problem comes from not trusting the corporate world. We know vaguely that they want something from us, but what is it? And what happens to us if we give it? Is this really a pact with the devil?

I had a call from a woman working in a political organization asking if she could pick my brain. Her organization was putting on a large special event and they wanted a corporate sponsor. I immediately recommended a large auto company which had approached a local organizer offering to underwrite an entire event. "Oh, no," she said. "That won't work. They invest in South Africa."

"Oh no," she said. "That won't work."

When is it appropriate to say no to corporate money? It is frustrating to have to limit the universe of potential donors for any reason. The problem with accepting money from corporations at odds with your organization's mission is that it makes you look like a hypocrite. Are you being bought out? Co-opted? Used? I once had a very successful fundraiser, and a good progressive man, tell me that there's no such thing as dirty money. "All money is dirty. We take it, put it to good use, and it becomes clean!"

Several years ago a gay and lesbian organization in California was offered a large grant by Coors beer. In addition to making controversial foreign investments, Coors had been accused of discriminating against gays by using lie detector tests in hiring. The gay and lesbian community had responded with a boycott, which, by the way, made AnheuserBusch very happy. In any case, the dilemma: Coors wanted to give the money in exchange for very high visibility around the gift. The organization struggled with it. They were broke and it would have been a nice piece of change. In the end, they said no.

What if they had said yes? They could have explained that they were not being co-opted. They even might have been able to strike a deal that would have enabled them to see Coors hiring practices for themselves. They might have been given permission to go to Colorado and give sensitivity classes on gay and lesbian issues for the management of Coors. They also might have lost a good percentage of their donors, volunteers and clients who would not wait for the explanation but just bolt out of sympathy to the boycott.

I believe that there is such a thing as "dirty money" if it is a gift with so many nasty strings that it causes you to unravel some of the good you've done in building your donor base. But rather than casting a suspicious eye on corporate sponsorship, I ask

How To Lose Donors Like Crazy

Tip #3: *When you sit down in his office with a prospect who is a corporate executive, be sure that your first remark is, "And so, what do you do here?"*

you to take a deep breath and think about how you might work with a corporation to build a partnership. If the aforementioned automobile company had been approached with partnership in mind, it is just possible that a give-and-take of ideas and politics could have resulted in some forward movement: understanding of the other's position, and possibly a new way to work together.

In fact, social services are losing ground in attracting corporate gifts. Corporate giving to the arts is on the rise. I believe that this is partly because corporations want clean and sexy exposure and want not to be associated with hunger, pain and death. The arts also make it very easy for a corporation to give. They put the corporation in the program, in their advertising, and they have an easy time putting corporate executives on their Boards. They are not plagued with having to worry about looking like hypocrites: they take no political stand, so the politics of a corporation is neither here nor there.

(I must note here, however, that things are somewhat different in other countries. A renowned dance troupe in Hong Kong recently revolted when their governing Board wanted to accept sponsorship from a tobacco company. They felt that they could not, in good conscience, even seem to be promoting smoking. The sponsorship was turned down.)

Social services and environmental groups, I am afraid, get caught in the trap of not **wanting** to understand corporate motives for giving. Corporations are often seen as "the enemy"

Think about how you might work with a corporation to build a partnership.

The arts make it easy for corporations to give.

55

by organizations struggling to feed people who have been abandoned by corporations, provide day care for children who are being ignored by corporations, clean up rivers being polluted by corporations, and compete with corporations for the last open space to build low cost housing. Then to turn around and smile and ask for money from the corporate sector, the same sector hyper-sensitive about its image and yet working day and night to keep "do-gooders" from ruining markets with boycotts and rumors... It's a jungle out there.

The whole prospect of creating a partnership, a dialogue, with corporations seems too much to ask of struggling non-profits. Board meeting after Board meeting, all across America, you will hear social services and environmentalists say, "We are cost-efficient, passionate about our work and absolutely essential... so why aren't people throwing money at us?"

Why? The wall that is going up between non-arts non-profits and corporate America is very destructive. It is a wall of ignorance and misguided self-righteousness. This will come as quite a shock to many non-profits, but THERE IS NO ENEMY! If it is your job to save the whales, get in your rubber boats and block the whalers. But don't forget to have armies of volunteers on shore educating everyone they can find about why the whales should be saved. This includes the whalers, their ship owners, and the governments that let them sail. If the people responsible for whaling won't listen, get five thousand people to stand up with you. Five hundred thousand.

It's a jungle out there.

"Why aren't people throwing money at us?'

Then look around at who is standing up with you. Get all of their names and phone numbers and make sure that you ask them to go one step further and write a check to make this important work happen. I once worked with an advocacy group struggling to raise money. I explained about "building your base". Finally the light bulb went on: "We have 50,000 names on a petition in our office. Should we solicit them?" Not only **should** you solicit them, but if you don't, you are robbing them of the opportunity to write a check and make a difference in a cause you already know they care about.

So you and your army of believers are shouting the truth to the rest of the world. Make sure that you are shouting it especially to the non-believers because the minute you put your hands on your hips and say, "They're the enemy. We will not dialogue with them," you, and a good number of innocent whales, are dead. Greenpeace knows this. It is also one of the most successful advocacy **and** fundraising non-profits in the country. This lesson must be learned at every level of social action if progress is to be made, not only in terms of creating a fundraising partnership with corporate America, but politically as well.

Artists and Their Twentieth Century Patrons

Corporate donations to the arts are on the rise in spite of the fact that mergers, changes in tax laws, and little or no history of philanthropy are affecting corporate giving in general. Why

If you don't, you are robbing them.

How To Lose Donors Like Crazy

Tip #13: *As soon as you finish a fundraising campaign, be sure to throw out the names of the donors. The list will just clutter up the place.*

aren't health care, AIDS, or issues affecting the homeless getting their share of the pie?

Corporate executives have to answer to their stockholders for decisions about how to make and spend profits. Philanthropy is not understood in this society, as has been discussed previously: People who ask for money are vultures, bleeding hearts and worse, and the causes they espouse are whiny liberal do-gooder charities. But the arts have presented themselves to the corporate sector in a totally different light. They are not charity. They are high society playing and enjoying the good life. They are an opportunity to link the corporate name with the stars: Pavarotti, Picasso, Perlman, et al. No controversy. No angry stockholders. Just good business, smart advertising, high name recognition, and fun.

It may sound like I am putting this approach down, but I am not. Although cause-related marketing has come under attack in some fundraising quarters, I am encouraged by the ingenuity of the arts to "sell" a tour of great paintings to a dog food producer. I see the lavish advertising done by the corporate sponsors as a boost to the arts specifically and all non-profits peripherally. And the concept of having Visa cards available to support public television, and all of the wonderfully inventive linkages of the arts to corporate support are advances in the field of fundraising. Just as the first "a-thon" opened a new creative door to events, I believe that cooperation with the corporate sector will leverage more dollars to make the arts more stable.

I am encouraged by the ingenuity of the arts to "sell" a tour of great paintings to a dog food producer.

58

I also believe that as arts organizations become more sophisticated in their corporate fundraising, they will become more selective about who they will link their name to. I must admit that I probably would have voted against allowing a tobacco company to associate itself with my dance organization. I would not want up-and-coming young artists, and audiences, to hear that an association with smoking is okay. Taken to the extreme, would you take cause-related monies from a drug ring? From a toxic polluter? From Oliver North? But I am sure that this kind of consciousness will become more prevalent as arts groups become more sought-after and therefore more choosy.

The lesson to be learned by all non-profits from the arts' innovative approach to corporate funding is to keep your eye focused on what the **donor** needs, **all** donors. It is obvious when you look at the corporate-arts partnership. But it translates to individual donors as well. Do they want status? Are they interested in revitalizing their community, as in the Oakland Symphony example? Do they want to save the world? Is recognition important? Anonymity? The more you can know what's in it for the donor, the more likely you will be to satisfy his or her need and create a mutually satisfying partnership.

Attitudes Toward Government Money

Another trap that catches and holds many an unsuspecting non-profit is the entitlement myth. I spoke in Idaho several years

Keep your eyes focused on what the donor needs...all donors.

ago to a coalition of social service agencies. In case you haven't noticed, Idaho is not California. When mining and foresting left the state, so did the jobs. Stores are boarded up and people are truly sleeping on sidewalks in once vital towns. I wanted to talk about major gifts. I wanted to help them to design good community-based events that would bring neighbors together in positive ways. But they were distracted by their own anger over entitlement. In his luncheon speech, the local Congressman had reported on the losing struggle to get government support restored. Now, mind you, the federal government had stopped giving to non-profits in any significant way **years** before. In Idaho, that meant that a very important and secure rug was slowly and skillfully pulled from under the non-profits and the people they served. By the time the rug was finally completely gone, their instinct was to yell, "Thief!" They thought the rug was theirs. It wasn't.

They thought the rug was theirs.

There are untold numbers of non-profits around the country that believe they are entitled to government support, and can make a good argument for their case. Most non-profits are taking care of Americans who have no place else to turn. Our tax dollars go to provide welfare. But it is the non-profit sector that provides the free or extremely low-cost services that allow people on welfare to get health care, food, and day care so that they can go out and find jobs. Non-profits do what governments in other countries do. As a matter of fact, many non-profits do what **this** government once did.

Many non-profits do what this government once did.

I worked in a community clinic that counted on government

60

money. Making the shift to fundraising and grant-writing was very painful. We felt like orphaned children. But that problem was ours. Counting on any funding, especially government money, is the most foolish thing a non-profit can do. Ask the libraries and public schools. If you are in the fix of having counted on any funding and you feel betrayed because you were entitled to that money, I will use my best counseling skills on you: Get over it. As Bev Galley says, it's time to pull up your socks and go on.

The most dangerous part about entitlement is when non-profits become so angry at the loss of their money that they are unable to act. They become paralyzed with self-righteous indignation. And they spend so much time shaking their collective fists at Washington or their state capitol that they lose sight of the fact that they're going broke and there are people out there who care and would write checks, attend events, and volunteer to help.

Several years ago, a community in the low-income Sierra foothills needed a fire truck. They held an event and every man, woman and child in that community came out and contributed. They raised enough money to buy the truck, and the other good news is: that fire truck is theirs. And the fires fought with that truck are put out with the love and caring, five dollars at a time, of the entire community.

I want to argue that, rather than bemoan the loss of government monies, we should celebrate. Governmental support for non-profits is:

If you are in the fix of having counted on any funding, and you feel betrayed because you were entitled to that money, get over it!

There are people out there who care and would write checks.

That fire truck is theirs.

- ❖ Quirky, shifting with every political breeze.
- ❖ So full of strings it might more aptly be called a quartet.
- ❖ Expensive. The reporting requirements are ridiculously bureaucratic and time-consuming.
- ❖ Hard to get. Governmental agencies love to pit non-profits against each other for the crumbs. "Sure, we'll give to the handicapped. The seniors will just have to cut back on their food consumption, that's all."
- ❖ Political! Lobbying, which non-profits are restricted from doing by the government, is essential if you want government monies!

The only really reliable source of funds for non-profits is the community. If people love you and write checks, and you take care of them, communicate with them and thank them, they will keep writing checks. The checks will be bigger every year, and they will thank **you** for doing the good work you are doing!

CHAPTER THREE
So, What is Fundraising, Anyway?

Terrifying! Necessary. Fun? Mysterious. There must be a book of right answers...

For some, fundraising feels so much like begging that they cannot bring themselves to do it. Actually, for many people, the little seed of "Oh, no, I don't want to do this..." is fertilized by fears that asking for money really **is** begging, and therefore beneath them. It is this misconception that keeps most people from venturing into fundraising. After all, who wants to be considered a beggar? If this is your, or your volunteers', problem, what you need is an attitude adjustment.

What you need is an attitude adjustment.

Something of Value

Start by thinking about why the work your organization is doing is of value. What is it about your program that makes you feel warm and satisfied? Even if you are a paid staff member, I know that it is certainly more than your undersized pay check that makes you feel good about the work you have chosen to do. Is it the look on a child's face when she listens to an aria? Is it seeing a news story about adults mentoring their low-income, troubled young friends? Is it seeing a puppy light up the face of a wheelchair-bound senior?

Fundraising starts with the recognition that the work you are doing is something of value. If you are having trouble identifying that value for your organization, fundraising will be difficult if not impossible for you. You can either push yourself to find the value there, or go elsewhere to fundraise.

If the "value" that you identify with your program is placed in the left-hand scale, in the right-hand scale you can place something else of value: Money. The "M" word. In your mind, see the value of the program and the value of the money balancing perfectly: **the good things happening for people are equal to the money that makes those good things happen.** Or picture that wonderful old ad for corporate sponsorship of the arts: the ballerina is on point, held up at the waist by a man in a three-piece suit. The money makes the program happen, and in the scheme of things, the money and the program are equal.

If your organization is deifying the program, feeling holy and wonderful about its existence, and decrying the fact that they have to lower themselves to go out and find the money to make it happen, what you are witnessing is The Begging Gap. I want you to hear once more that **fundraising is nothing like begging.** In begging, one person asks another person for money, and the giver gets nothing in return, except perhaps rid of the beggar. Fundraising is providing an opportunity for people in the community to give something of value to make something of value happen. They are the secure hands at the ballerina's waist. They make the art/health care/advocacy happen just as surely as the dancers/doctors/raft pilots do! It is a partnership of the highest order. Those check-writers get, in

The money and the program are equal.

The Begging Gap

return, to feel as good about the work you are doing as you do, because without them, you cannot do your work. Not everyone can be on the front line providing services, painting scenery, wiping runny noses and the rest of it. And not everyone can volunteer to be on your Board. They do not have the skills or the inclination. But do not presume that they do not care.

Having trouble getting started in fundraising because of your attitude leads to either procrastination or negative fundraising: "You wouldn't want to give, would you?" This leads to the misconception that people in the community do not care about the work you are doing and fundraising will not work. As soon as your organization decides that fundraising will not work, you are absolutely correct. At that point, it will not work.

As soon as your organization decides that fundraising will not work, you are absolutely correct: it won't.

Back up and look at the attitude of the key people in your organization. How do they feel about the work you are doing? Are they on fire? If so, you are ready to fundraise. If they stay in touch with their passion for the work you are doing, asking for money will be easy. If they are not on fire, you need a different group of people to do fundraising for you.

There is a saying in fundraising: without commitment, no strategy will work. Where there's commitment, there's no strategy that **won't** work.

Without commitment, no strategy will work. With commitment, there's no strategy that won't work.

Now take a look at the role the community plays in your non-profit. No matter what kind of work you are doing, your organization exists because the need for that work exists. That

65

is how non-profits are different from for-profit businesses. We are not in business to stimulate the need for the work we do. The need exists outside of us and we are responding to it. We do not need to keep reminding the community of their need for our widgets. They have a need for health services, day care, environmental protection and the arts. If the need stops, the organization either goes away or focuses on another need. That's what happened with March of Dimes. They addressed the problem of polio. Once polio was cured, they re-grouped and decided to focus on birth defects.

Ownership

Since the need for the work we do emanates from the community, good community-based fundraising means giving people an opportunity to write a check to meet their own need, to solve a problem or provide a service that is needed within their own community. Good fundraising completes the circle. It gives the community the rightful ownership of issues that are their own.

Good fundraising gives the community rightful ownership of issues.

Ownership is a big and very important word in fundraising. By "own" I mean the feeling that you get when you write a check for a non-profit and open the newspaper and see an article about them. You say "Wow! I wonder what they're up to?" and you feel connected to that organization. You have invested your money in their work. It is that feeling of connectedness that you want to spread all over the community.

"Wow! I wonder what they're up to now?"

It is the partnership of the non-profit with the community to meet their own needs that is at the heart of fundraising.

New organizations often think that all that they need is "one big angel" to give the money to make it all happen. Even if it were possible to find such a person or funding source, there are some real problems with this model:

❖ Control. If one person is funding the whole thing, they will surely want some say in things like who you hire and what your brochure looks like.

❖ Stability. Unless this is a gift made in perpetuity, your organization will constantly be poised and ready for the funder to pull out the rug, fold up their tent and head for more fertile grounds.

❖ Who is your master? The positive model for non-profits is: services flow from need, and fundraising flows from services. The need in this model is the need of the community. Where does the need of the angel funder fit? If the community is speaking to you of one need, and the angel is speaking of another, whose call do you answer?

If your organization looks like a giant slab of concrete, think about that slab with hundreds, even thousands of support posts holding it up. That is what an organization with community buy-in looks like. It is stable, rooted in the community, and if some of the donors need to go away, more will replace them and your organization will be more stable every year.

When you go out into the community to talk with potential donors, stay focused on the fact that you raise money for people, not projects. If you are having trouble meeting payroll, that is your Board's problem. If you want to start up new counseling services for seniors, the key word in that phase is not "start-up", but "seniors". Be ready to talk about who the seniors are and what is happening in their lives. What will happen for them if they get the counseling you are offering? What will happen for the neighbors, families and friends of those seniors if they get the counseling?

The key word is not "start-up".

The old chestnut "people give to people" is absolutely reliable. People not only give to people when asked, but people give to the people your program is helping. The only crisis you may take out to the community is the crisis that would occur in the lives of the people you serve if they were not to get the service you are providing: a generation growing up without performing arts, a whole species of birds erased from the earth, latch-key children returning to empty apartments to fend for themselves.

People give to people.

The "crisis" of your bookkeeping department does not make a good, imaginative, exciting opening argument. It used to be, when I first began fundraising in 1976, that you could say, "We have to have $5000 to keep our doors open!" and get it. Now it seems that donors are more sophisticated or more worn down by non-profits screaming poverty and doom. They tell us now, "Close them... and write when you get work." Step out into the community to fundraise with a positive attitude and an invitation for the community to join you in the wonderful work

68

you are doing. Once they hear your message and are thinking about making a gift, of course they can know everything about you. They should be cordially invited to look at your Certified Public Audit, have a tour of your facilities, even look through your books if they want to. You, as a non-profit, are an open book. You exist to meet the needs of the community, and the community has every right to know how their investment will be handled. I have also found that the more open and available you are to prospective donors who have questions about your organization, the more likely you are to get the gift. They do not want you to be IBM. They just don't want you to be the next non-profit to make the front pages because of mismanagement.

"Close them...and write when you get work."

Crisis

Think about crisis. Most non-profits exist hand-to-mouth. I worked with a fairly new non-profit this week that said, "We have enough money to get through the next three months." Another group I am helping said, "We have $8000 in the bank and will have to start drawing down on that this month." They are seventeen years old. The "crisis" of running out of money is standard operating procedure in most non-profits. As a matter of fact, you should realize that non-profit does NOT mean no profit. It means that individuals may not profit from the organization's work. You **may** end the year with black ink in your books. You SHOULD end the year with black ink in your books! I recommend that every organization follow the lead of the Girl Scouts and shoot for having one year's operating

...running out of money is standard operating procedure.

budget in the bank as a buffer.

The "crisis" of continually running out of money, permanently worrying about making payroll, has several outcomes:

❖ This state of being can be habit forming in a negative way. Anyone who hangs around non-profits for any period of time would assume that hand-to-mouth is the way business is supposed to be carried out. If EVERYONE does it, then it must be right.

❖ Worrying about making payroll is distracting. It affects sleep, work, fun, friendships, and burns out very good, useful, dedicated folks.

❖ It makes you a very poor investment. Donors have the right to know everything about you before they write a check, including, and perhaps especially, the state of your finances. Not knowing where the money will come from next month says that you are a very poor manager indeed, and if the prospective donor ran her or his business that way, they would soon be out of business. Again, the donor's interest is not in helping you, but in the people you serve.

The Chinese symbol for crisis is the combination of two symbols: danger and opportunity. Of course the danger of a money crisis is what totally preoccupies us. But think for a moment of the "opportunity" part. The opportunity within the danger is the chance to take a deep breath, pull up your socks and take a leap beyond the old way of doing things into a more stable way to operate.

You may not fundraise from a crisis mentality. It just isn't a good argument and it makes you look flaky. But we keep doing it, don't we? More than half of the direct mail appeals that are sent out for money begin with "Dear Friend: Help!"

The only crisis that you may take out to the community when you are asking for money is the crisis that would affect the community and the people you serve if you did not exist: No poetry in the schools, no voice to defend the eagles, no shelter for battered women and children, no affordable housing in the community.

You may remind people of the important role you play in making this a better place to live and work. You must tell the truth to prospective donors and offer up your fiscal reality for inspection. But you may not insist that you will die without their help. No one wants to write the last $500 check to pay the bookkeepers to close the books.

Walls

In fundraising, there are two kinds of walls. The first one is real and has to do with having enough time to do the event, enough money for postage, enough volunteers for the membership drive. This wall can be scaled, and probably will be scaled over and over as you run through your fundraising activities for the year. But the second wall is of more concern to me. It is higher and wider and very difficult to get over. It is the wall of fear.

The only crisis you may take out to the community is the crisis that would happen if your clients were not served.

Why "fear of fundraising"? Rejection, of course. The thought of getting up enough courage to ask someone for money only to have them laugh or get angry and say no is enough to keep us from even **beginning** to fundraise.

I find the wall of fear showing up in all kinds of places. One very common place for it to show itself is in a Board meeting when the members finally agree to go out and ask for large gifts. Then they qualify it by announcing, "But I'm not going to ask my friends. I don't want to ruin good friendships." And someone else adds, "And I'm not going to ask our clients to give. That would embarrass them." And a third voice says, "Well, I don't think we should ask our volunteers. We rely on them and if we ask them for money they'll go away..." People with money are eliminated because the Board is sure that they would never get in to see them. And people without money are eliminated because "not everyone can give". Pretty soon every human being in the universe is eliminated, and fundraising is over before it starts.

Do not say no for people. They do that just fine all by themselves. If you hear anyone say no for anyone else, understand that what is going on there has more to do with fear than anything else.

If you buy what I am saying about fundraising being an opportunity for people to feel as good about the good work your organization is doing as you do, then saying no for anyone is robbing them of the chance to provide something of value and thereby make something of value happen. The discomfort experienced here is not the discomfort of the prospective donor at all. That person isn't even in the room. The discomfort present when someone says no for someone else is completely the ASKER'S discomfort at the prospect of having to approach the person being discussed.

The Ask

Far too many discussions about going out to do face-to-face fundraising stop right there. "YUCK! This feels awful! I can't do this." I could probably name fifty organizations that actually have major donor prospect lists, adequate materials and a great case to make for someone writing a large check, but the volunteers sink the ship by feeling too scared to make it happen.

When you are trying to move a group of people to go out and ask for money, your major concern should be: Where is their comfort level, and how can I raise it?

"Yuck! This feels awful!"

Start by acknowledging that ASKING FOR MONEY IS SCARY! As you do more asking, it becomes a little easier. But eyeball-to-eyeball fundraising is not natural for most human beings, and once that is acknowledged out loud, your askers can take a deep breath and move a step closer to getting over their wall.

The second layer of realization has to do with asking friends for money. It is a fact of life that the majority of people in this world are more comfortable asking strangers for money than asking friends. But we usually approach a Board by telling them to "Just go out and ask your friends!" TERROR! AGONY! GUILT! AVOIDANCE! Acknowledge out loud that, if your askers are uncomfortable in asking their friends, they are in the majority in this world. Review "Don't say no for anyone," reminding them that they feel great about giving money and time to your organization, and all they are doing is offering the same "feels great" to the rest of the community by **letting** them write checks. Then encourage them to turn in their friends. If they go through their rolodexes and write down the names, addresses, and phone numbers of people they know who could give $500 or more, making a note of how much to ask for and how each person feels about the issue you are addressing, this becomes a great potential donor list.

The absolute best way to have the people on the list approached is to have the contact person do the ask. But if that is too uncomfortable, the second best way is to have the contact person turn the list over to a fellow asker, briefing the asker on who the people are and the best way to approach them, and then opening the door. By opening the door I mean having the contact person call the people they know one at a time, starting with the absolute most likely giver, and do the following:

1) Remind them, or tell them for the first time, of his or her involvement with the organization **and** that he or she is a donor;

How to Avoid Fundraising

I met with the President of a human services organization which has since gone out of business. This man was himself extremely wealthy but reluctant to tap his resources for this group. He took the executive director and me to a very expensive restaurant to discuss his hot new idea for fundraising and get our feedback. He began by explaining that they needed $53,000 or the organization would fold. (I still believe that he could have written the check himself and charged it to petty cash.) But his great idea was to contact all the newspapers in the area and get them to run a free

2) Tell the organization's story, keeping in mind who the prospect is and what she or he cares about;

3) Advise the prospect that the contact has given his or her name to Susy Smith on the Board, and Susy will be calling to make an appointment to ask the prospect to join them as a major donor, and the contact hopes that the prospect will meet with Susy to hear her story.

Of course, Susy trades lists, having her friends followed up on by the person whose list she is working, and she briefs the asker and opens the door in the same way.

The final acknowledgement used to raise the comfort level of prospective askers is in fact the most powerful. I find it extremely helpful in training askers to remind them that if they do their homework and know who they are asking, know that the amount they are requesting is the right amount, and know how the prospect feels about the issue, and if they call or write to ask for an appointment, stating very clearly that a major gift will be requested, AND THE PROSPECT AGREES TO MEET WITH THE ASKER, from then on it's only a matter of how large the gift will be. The prospect will not agree to meet with an asker, and then sit down and say, "Oh, darn, I just remembered... I hate you."

People often get stuck on "the ask". If the appointment is set up with all expectations laid out on the table, sitting down at that table with the prospect is not so much an "ask" as it is a coming

ad for the organization with a coupon "asking 53,000 people to send in $1." The problem with this strategy is that advertising does not substitute for good fundraising. Even if he could get every newspaper in the area to run a coupon for free, the reader could simply not see the ad and turn the page. Or the reader could see it, think it was interesting, and turn the page. If the reader really got hooked by the ad and decided to send in $1, he would have to get up, and find the check book, a pen, an envelope, a stamp, and scissors. Then, he'd have to sit back down and mutilate his newspaper. If you remember that you have to make giving as easy as you can for your prospects, you will see that this is not the greatest of strategies.

to terms. The prospect knows why the asker is coming! You've made that clear in the approach. I have found that I am more comfortable in putting the amount out there in the beginning, either over the telephone or in the letter: "I want to meet with you to ask you to give $5000 this year." There! Phew! It's said. If you have done your homework and know that's the right amount for this prospect, the prospect will not faint. Often times the prospect will say, "I don't know about that amount." And I'll say, "That's fine. Let's meet and talk about it." At least the prospect knows what ballpark I'm playing in. At the face-to-face meeting, then, it's a matter of answering questions, listening, and repeating the ask. If I actually get this far with a prospect, I always come away with a check or a pledge.

Mill Valley Community Schools Foundation exists to raise money for the "extras" in public school: science, art, music, physical education, grants to encourage teachers, etc. I joined the Board because I had two children in the schools, and they made me Chair of Major Gifts. The ED, Penny, was thrilled, and said, "This is fine but you'll never get me to ask for money." Three years later, as I was leaving the Board, Penny had a hot prospect. She finally agreed to go with me on the solicitation and make the presentation if I would do The Ask. This was an older man whose children had gone through the schools. Penny decided I should ask for 10K a year for five years. Penny, as she always does, made a very eloquent presentation. She then hesitated, and blurted, "Burke has something to ask you." As I began to tell him about the

The Ask

There! Phew! It's said.

Board's involvement and major gifts, and endowing arts and sciences, Penny sat with an uncomfortable grin glued to her face. I said, "And so, we'd like you to consider giving 10K a year for five years. What do you think?" This was followed by a fairly long silence, yet there was only one uncomfortable person at the table. It was neither me nor the prospect. We had done our homework, and we knew this was the right person and the right amount. But this was Penny's first encounter with the Silence. We wound up getting $2,500/year for five years, and we were disappointed. But I want you to know two things about this Ask:
1) At the next Board meeting we were virtually carried around the table on Board members' shoulders; and 2) Soon after that Penny said, "So, who are we going to Ask next?"

Telling the Truth

In the creation of this relationship between the donor and the organization, it is very important that the organization is willing to be a totally open book. So you step out to meet the donor with your best foot forward, ready to explain why the work you are doing in the community is something of value. Then you answer the prospect's questions totally honestly. You do not have to be absolutely perfect to attract a gift, but you do have to be absolutely honest. I have found it helpful to draw the donor into a discussion of how your problems could be fixed. Perhaps they have the solution. But in any case, they have the right to know what state you are in before they invest in your work.

I've encountered a good number of non-profit organizations over the years that operate like the CIA. Their books are closed and secret and so are their Board meetings. I have even heard tell of non-profit Boards that do not allow staff, even the Executive Director, access to the Board members. What on earth could they have to hide? These are not just the large non-profits, by the way. Little guys sometimes cloak themselves in secrecy, too.

Awhile back NASA launched a space probe in secrecy. When a Congressperson was asked why it had been kept a secret, he said, "I guess they think it's more fun that way."

Your organization may think it's more fun that way, and perhaps it makes them feel more important if they have some non-secret to protect, but I urge you to operate your non-profit organizations in a very open and inviting manner. All non-profits exist to serve the common good The community will be more inclined to get involved, donating time and money, if they feel welcomed into the process.

"I guess they think it's more fun that way."

So You Want To Be A Fundraiser

Fundraising is not popular in this society. I recently presented a training in the different techniques of fundraising to the Board of a health organization. Direct mail? "No way. I hate getting all that junk mail." Telemarketing? "Phone calls? I always hang right up on them." Special event? "I hate those rubber chicken dinners." Face-to-face solicitations? "People with money won't want to give to **us.**" If you are not going to ask them face-to-face, and the mail and telephone are out, how **do** you propose getting the money?

Too often non-profits decide that the answer to their prayers is to hire a "Fundraiser", give her a telephone and typewriter, and have her call the Board when the money starts to flow in. I'm afraid it doesn't work this way. A professional fundraiser, usually called Director of Development, does not raise money. At least that is not her primary duty. She may write grants that bring in some money, or organize direct mail appeals that work, or be part of the asking team, but the vital role of this very important staff person is to keep fundraising on track. This means:

1) Keeping the Board and volunteer fundraisers motivated, trained, and out there asking for money;

2) Thanking everyone!

3) Making sure that the donor records are impeccably kept;

4) Developing a year-long fundraising plan that has a place for every volunteer;

5) Thanking everyone!

6) Identifying new volunteers in the community and working with the staff and Board to bring them in;

7) Thanking everyone!

A professional fundraiser, usually called Director of Development, does not raise money.

I am glad to say that I am finally seeing a trend toward paying these dedicated people what they're worth. Experienced fundraisers are now beginning to earn more than Executive Directors. This is good news because good fundraisers are able to cut to the chase, guiding organizations away from foolish strategies and leading them in keeping their eyes fixed firmly on the prize.

I often tell students that they need to put on "fundraising blinders" when they are looking at how their organization functions, or doesn't function. Anything that gets in the way of fundraising must be moved aside. Sometimes that means hurting peoples' feelings by forcing them to be team players or leave. Sometimes that means exposing very sensitive feelings and risking getting hurt.

Stay alert to dangerous situations. People who promise to give and/or raise money but always have an excuse ("Oh, I forgot my list..." "I'm getting ready to go on a trip. I'll do it when I get back...") will undermine fundraising. Set a deadline in your own mind for how soon they need to deliver. If the deadline passes with no results, write them off. People who have a negative word for every fundraising idea ("That will never work because...") will drag down the entire team, or undermine the possibility of ever putting together an effective team. You must move them aside. People who never do any fundraising but are anxious to call a "let's-cut-back-the-programs" meeting are leading your organization astray. Replace them with can-do people.

...eyes on the prize

...fundraising blinders

People who have a negative word for every idea will undermine the entire team.

Remembering why you exist, who you are serving as your first priority, will bring you back on track and make moving people out of your way easier.

The person who is responsible for fundraising must also have her or his priorities very together. That person's first priority is the donor. That is who **you** primarily serve, along with the fundraising volunteers and the Board. That means that each donor is cared for as personally as possible. Letters and phone calls keep them informed and stroked. They are asked once a year for an appropriate amount. They are acknowledged publicly, if that is their desire. This caretaking job is just like the work you do to keep your personal life in order: remembering birthdays, favorite foods, names of grandchildren. Remember which wife is the current one and which is the ex. Be ready to recall pieces of previous conversations. Be impeccable with the details and people will appreciate it.

If the person in charge of fundraising —you— does not get distracted by the politics, the power struggles, the confusion and general chaos of the non-profit but always stays focused on the **donor** as first priority, fundraising will grow.

When you're ready to make a leap into a more sophisticated mode of operations, these goals, along with a good set of fundraising blinders, will help you to jump. You **want** to bring in energized community people. You **need** to create a major gifts campaign. You **know** that you cannot subsist hand-to-mouth for one more day without exploding. How does your

Each donor is cared for as personally as possible.

organization make that leap?

It starts with attitude. How do you feel about hurting peoples feelings? You need to answer that question honestly because in order to make the leap, you will undoubtedly step on some toes. Do you have some staff or Board members who believe that a non-profit social service agency needs to look poor to "prove" to the world that they're doing their job? Do you have Board members who refuse to give and raise money? Is your arts organization fatalistic about fundraising because the issue isn't life-and-death? Is the staff refusing to participate in fundraising? Those people are standing in the way of progress.

"Attitude" in fundraising means being clear about how you feel about money, both having it and spending it. "Having it" has to do with asking for it without apologizing. "Spending it" has to do with fundraising because if you intend to attract major donors you will need quality materials to represent you to the prospect, as well as well-produced newsletters and the capability of thanking donors appropriately. It takes money to do these things. If you or your cohorts are stuck in thinking of fundraising as begging, keep reading this book. Your attitude is your main stumbling block to forward progress.

How can your organization make the leap?

Do you have Board members who refuse to give and raise money? These people are standing in the way of progress.

"Why should anyone want to give us money?"

"I know people with money, but I would never ask them to give here."

"The Board gives their time. It's too much to ask for money, too."

"There's too much competition in fundraising. It won't work."

"Any amount you can give will be wonderful."

Attitude.

How To Lose Donors Like Crazy

Tip #9: Direct mail requests must never mention money. With direct mail you are seeking support and giving the donor an update. Enclose a return envelope.

A Word About Fundraising Brochures

A brochure for a non-profit organization has, at its best, just enough words to make the reader want to know more. It is NOT

❖ your Master's thesis

❖ a thorough and complete history of your organization

❖ full of pictures of the backs of peoples' heads

❖ printed in minuscule type

❖ impossible to open/read/understand

❖ written in "social worker" English:
"Our multi-dimensional program was developed to meet specific needs of the community. The wide range of programs and approaches provides the flexibility to use all or part of any program to meet the individual needs of each client. It is possible for clients to develop a truly individualized prescriptive strategy within a comprehensive yet appropriate operative framework."

-copied directly from a real life brochure. I've had the brochure for so long that I do not remember what this organization does for people. Can you figure out what it might be?

❖ so artsy-colorful that the human eye rejects reading it

❖ a request for money

❖ a list of current players, Board or staff, because as soon as one or more of these players leave, the brochure is obsolete.

Brochures should not be expected to stand on their own. Stay focused on the brochure as introduction. Create a brochure that gives the reader a taste of who you are, your voice and face, your philosophy and aspirations.

Yes, I know that you do not have all the money in the world. Yes, I know how expensive a good brochure can be. Certainly you should be frugal, sensible and down-to-earth. For precisely those reasons and others I urge you to produce one brochure for each audience you wish to reach. In the long run, this strategy is cheaper than trying to do, once and for all, the definitive brochure that tells how to use the program, offers membership/major gift options/corporate in-kind needs, a pie chart, list of staff members with credentials, and has four paragraphs that open with, "In 1948, our Founder had a dream..." This brochure will be cheaper to print than the five or six brochures you really need, but it will be extremely expensive if it sits in boxes in your office because no one wants to read it.

If nothing else, you must have at least one fundraising brochure. The purpose of this lovely document is to give the reader the clear sense that you are ready and willing to accept donations and put them to good use because you've thought it all through. A good fundraising brochure DOES NOT

- contain inserts that fall out when you open it
- include a coupon for the prospect to clip and send in because once the coupon is clipped, the brochure is mutilated and the prospect tosses it in the garbage.
- ask for money
- focus on more than three ways to give.

The fundraising brochure accompanies an asker on a face-to-face ask, or it goes in a letter that requests money. In order for you to get the most our of your fundraising brochure, it must be beautiful and readable so that it does NOT get tossed out but passed from prospect hand to prospect hand ("Hey! Look at this!"). The opportunities for giving within one brochure must be fairly narrow so that the reader feels that the brochure has been written for his or her needs. It you start with membership and go through major gifts and deferred giving, that's plenty for one brochure. If you go onto corporate opportunities and loaned executives, the membership/major gift prospect will realize that you are not talking to him or her and **stop reading.**

A good fundraising brochure DOES include
- great photos
- lots of white/open space so that the words do not appear jammed
- opportunities for the donor
- your address and phone number featured prominently
- soothing, warm colors (unless you're a museum of modern art)
- a BRIEF explanation of how the money is used and what your program does to enrich the world
- up-beat, readable phrases with bullets, or very short sentences

You can save money on a series of brochures by doing them all in the same three colors, same paper, and running them all at once on the press.

gray textured paper, with the Board brochure plum on the outside and black inside, and the Technical Assistance brochure black on the outside and plum inside. They are distinctly different, but they complement and work with each other.

Make sure that at least three people proof your brochure. Years ago I produced 10,000 brochures for a social service agency featuring the wrong phone number! Not learning my lesson, I went on to create my first business brochure. One of the services I offered was development of "effective brochrues". The best way to proof anything is to read it backwards, word by word.

How To Focus On Fundraising Priorities

It is true that there may be many good reasons to conduct a fundraising activity: money, good PR, recognition. But just as the fundraiser must know how to focus on the donor, the organization must focus on **why** a particular fundraising activity is happening, and then make sure that it happens.

Have you ever done a special event, at the end of which you sighed and commented, "Oh, well, it was good PR." That oft-quoted sentence means that the organization was shooting for another target and missed, and most likely that target was cash.

The best was to insure that you hit the target you need to hit with a fundraising activity is to begin the activity by answering the question, "What do we want to have happen here?" Make a list. How much money do you want to make? And how little can you tolerate making? Are you doing this to honor someone? If so, what is the best way to honor that particular person? If you are aiming for good PR, what media are the best suited to your purposes? Are you trying to cultivate new donors with this event? What is the best way to turn them on to your organization? Do you want to educate people? Will your target audience pick up and carry home brochures or do you need a different medium for your message? What is the minimum gift you will consider as "major"? How will you honor those givers? Do you need to upgrade your image in the community? Would a special event with a new "look" help?

"Oh, well, it was good PR."

Hit the target you want to hit.

87

If you have two or three goals, especially for a special event, and you keep your eyes focused on those goals, you will undoubtedly meet them. Once again, do not get distracted by frustrated Board members, needy volunteers, or demanding administration. Write down your goals, put them where you will see them every day, and keep your fundraising machine rolling toward success.

CHAPTER FOUR
The "M" Word

Social Services and Money: Getting it in Perspective

Focusing again on attitudes toward money, let's look at non-profits that deal with the human question. There is a different style to these non-profits, much different from arts organizations or advocacy groups. Where the arts "don't do money", and advocacy groups (lobbying, protection of liberties, animal rights, etc.) struggle to show what the donated money actually buys, with social services it is internally politically correct to look, and in some cases to actually be, poor. Money is suspect. And people with money are co-opters, wheeler-dealers and worse.

Think about the effect this has on donor and volunteer development. Several years ago I actually had a very long conversation with folks at a women's clinic about whether they should even seek people with money and contacts to be on their Board. And they were broke! They feared what all such organizations fear: that people with money will "take over". It is a power issue. I must ask such an organization, "Take over **what?**" They have 12 cents in the bank, Board meetings take five hours and deal with survival, the whole place needs painting and the furniture is falling apart. Is this take-over material?

Fundraising is a **program** just like Thursday night clinic, parent

**How To Lose
Donors Like Crazy**

Tip #10: *Make sure you have your donors keep the names of their friends and acquaintances to themselves. And if a major donor offers to introduce you to a tennis partner who owns a major law firm, say you are too busy.*

Is this take-over material?

education, English classes and the rest. Because there is so much more to fundraising than just the money, it is possible to look at the side benefits from the perspective of what fundraising does for the community. If you do an event, you are bringing the community together for fun and giving them a sense of coming together to do good. When you invite people to write checks through direct mail, you are giving them a chance to make your organization happen. The need that your organization is meeting in the community is not your need, or your clients' need, alone. The need is the community's need: to protect puppies, instruct bicycle riders, plant trees, whatever. You are acting in the name of the community to meet an endemic need. If you did not meet that need, someone else would have to do it. So good fundraising means allowing the community to write checks and solve a problem that is just as much theirs as it is that of the people you serve. It is, in fact, giving ownership back where it belongs: to the community.

The best that can happen in fundraising is that you build a team that includes all of the Board, the staff and the volunteers, and leaves room for the community to give and raise money.

If you leave poor people out of this equation, you are doing elitist fundraising. Everyone can give! I once worked with an agency that served runaway and thrownaway youth. They built a very powerful, monied Board but it was somewhat disconnected from the kids they served. In order to help the Board understand these children, one rainy day we took a tape recorder to the lobby where kids gathered to stay dry. We

Fundraising is a program, just like Thursday night clinic.

Everyone can give.

90

interviewed the kids, asking "How old are you?" Most, with squeaky little voices, fibbed "Eighteen." Where had they slept the night before? In abandoned cars, in doorways and under dumpsters. "How much money do you have in your pocket?" They had anywhere from eighteen cents to nineteen or twenty dollars. Now, these kids were hustlers, dealing drugs and selling their bodies to have enough food to eat. "The system" will not deal with you if you have no ID, and very few kids run away from home with their birth certificates. They were tough little kids. But then we asked, "If this clinic were in trouble, would you donate some money?" Not only did all of them volunteer all of their cash on a rainy day, but several of them were quite insistent that we take it. We asked them why they were so willing to help, and they said, "This Center has been there for me." That 18 cents equals the $40,000 a Board member was giving because it was all the child had. The $40,000 donor had millions, and the resources to accumulate even more. On that rainy day, that child certainly did not know where his next eighteen cents was coming from. If your client is left out of the circle of donors because he is poor, then you are saying that he can only receive the service, he cannot be part of solving the problem.

At the other end of the scale, you may not leave rich people out of the equation either. So you ask Ms Moneybags for $10,000 and she agrees to give it. Then what? The speculation here is, "What will she want in return?" Will she want to run your program? Tell you who to hire? Who to serve? The fear is that that $10,000 will be such a strong siren song that you will take it and give her whatever she wants.

What **does** she want, anyway? She definitely wants to be thanked appropriately: a warm letter, maybe a plaque, an invitation to the Major Donor Luncheon. She definitely wants to know that her money is doing some good. Be sure to keep her informed about the programs she is making possible, the clients her money is helping. But what does she **really** want? Chances are very good that it is not power. People who are power-hungry usually do not look to social service agencies to get their needs met. It is a much better bet that she has one or several of the following needs: to change the world, to feel good, to assuage her guilt, to give something back to society, to see her name on a major donor list or a wall, to publicize her business, to meet other major donors in her community, and so on. Furthermore, if she cares enough to make a very large contribution to your agency, I recommend that you consider putting her on your Board. She is already committed, and if she will bring her friends in as donors you will have the start of a successful major donor campaign.

The way to keep the balance of power equal on your Board when you bring on your first major donor is to be sure that every member is giving an equal gift. I do not mean "equal" in numerical size. That is not what counts. Setting the "Board gift" at $200 per year, or $25,000, is a big mistake. I have found that no matter what number you set, a third of the people you need on the Board will not be able to give that much and you will lose them. Another third will find the number just right. And

What does she want, anyway? Chances are very good that it is not power.

Setting the "Board gift" is a big mistake.

the final third will be laughing up their sleeves because they are getting off with such a small gift. The only way to have equality between Board members is to have them all give at the sacrificial level. Inevitably, this concept leads to a discussion of Board members' priorities: "But I serve on five Boards!" Theoretically, I believe it's possible to serve on more than one Board and love each "equally". But what I wish for your organization is to have a Board comprised of people for whom your non-profit is their **top** giving and volunteering priority. Then their commitment is a given.

To fully understand the import of this concept, think about the single largest gift you've ever given to a non-profit. Say it's $500. You may have had to pledge it, pay it in installments. But life went on. The kids got fed. The light bill got paid. For some people $5 is like that $500. It's a major commitment. For others, $50,000, or even $5,000,000 is like that $500. Life goes on. If each Board member is giving to the max, then all gifts are equal and your Board will not give more weight to what the "big donor" feels and says.

The trap that most social service agencies' solicitors fall into when it comes to major donors is the terror of asking someone for more money than they make in a year. Or three years. Or ever. Mr. Bigbucks comes into your clinic. You are wearing your standard uniform: blue jeans, sneakers, a wool sweater and plenty of turquoise jewelry. This is how your clients dress, and dressing any other way would make them uncomfortable. Mr. Bigbucks is wearing a cashmere jacket, shined wingtips, and a

If each Board member is giving the max, then all gifts are equal.

diamond pinky ring. You panic. How can you ask him to give the $5000 you had planned to ask him for when you are so obviously different?

Remember several things. Mr. Bigbucks dresses as he dresses because it is how everyone in **his** world looks. Dressing any other way would make the people he deals with very uncomfortable. In that you are equal. But he makes more money than you ever plan to make. And he is a mover and shaker in the community, a real power broker. Doesn't that make it impossible for you to ask? No. Realize that if you are giving to your organization at a sacrificial level, chances are very good that proportionately your gift is **larger** than the one you are asking him to make: proportionately, yours is probably a bigger sacrifice. Finally, I want you to know that if you are working, paid or unpaid, for a non-profit organization in this society at this time in our history, you are nothing less than a hero. **You** are taking care of the people who need care, giving of your time and energy, and probably not getting paid much at all, if anything. You are the mover and shaker. I defy anyone to identify another human being whose work is more important than yours.

Advocacy Groups: Taking Care of Yourselves

There is no doubt that advocacy groups are the most exciting and motivated groups around. Their issues propel them. Whatever issue they are espousing, they are constantly

94

What Color to Paint Your Clinic ... *Or, How to Look Really Poor and Needy Through Color*

It's time to paint your clinic. Given that all colors cost roughly the same, it is very important to put cost aside and consider the psychological messages that colors transmit.
Beige: *We're too poor and humble to be bright, but we're so drab that we must be doing wonderful work for the poor.*
White: *Clean. Very clean. Professional, sterile and pure. No parties here. No time for fun. Take off your clothes and stick out your tongue.*
Yellow: *Bright. Sunny. We're cheerful and we like children.*
Institutional Green: *We are so cost-efficient that we took the left-over paint from the prison.*

reminded how urgent it is: whales are still harpooned, rights are eroding, people still drink and drive, children are molested, immigrants pursued. The media keep them on track by reminding them of the whole universe of atrocities.

It is very rewarding on some levels to work with an advocacy group. They are now! They make a difference! They are true believers!

The down side of this kind of work is, unfortunately, very down. These groups are so very involved in their passionate work that they might:

❖ forget to thank anyone

❖ leave amenities like employee benefits and comfortable chairs to figure out tomorrow, which never arrives

❖ march into hostile camps with their chins thrust out as a matter of pride **or**

❖ believe that "angry" is an acceptable on-going facial expression.

Forgetting to thank people is **never** acceptable for any reason. In the case of advocacy groups, does it make sense to fight for what you believe in by using your volunteers and donors as battering rams? If you use up the human energy and dollars that fellow true believers are providing without providing for replenishing of those resources, eventually those comrades will take their time and money elsewhere. The replenishing is only a matter of thanking. Everyone wants to feel competent, appreciated and liked. If you are leaving your volunteers and donors feeling confused, ignored and not needed you are doing a disservice to everyone and to your cause.

In order to turn this situation around, please observe the following rules:

+ NOTICE and REMEMBER what people do and give.
+ SAY IT back to them..."Hey! I just heard you sent in a check for $100. That's great!" (This takes practice, but it's worth it.)
+ IDENTIFY them with their gift..."I'd like you to meet Joe. He spent last week collecting signatures for us and managed to get over 500!"
+ BUY yourself some note cards. Or better yet, get note cards printed with your organization's logo. Use them to send quick and personal thank you notes to people who are giving their precious resources to the cause.
+ THANK everyone officially, even if you have to write the letter for the President yourself and give it to her to sign.

I attended a meeting recently at which a volunteer was outlining how she planned to raise $2 million for the organization. She had brought a prospective donor with her to the meeting so that the prospect could see how well organized the campaign was. The fundraising volunteer, at a strategic point, told the group that she planned to give $5000 and that she had challenged the prospect to give another $5000. This was a totally unexpected turn of events. Yet not one person in the room responded. No one said, "Thank you!" or "That's great!"

The reason for this Awkward Silence was discomfort with money. Now remember, in this case the donor is very comfortable with revealing her gift. Our lack of comfort is what creates the awkwardness. Whose job is it to represent the organization and say thank you? When someone tells us something as personal as how much they will be giving, shouldn't we be embarrassed? As it happened, I, the "Consultant", jumped in and thanked her. Once I broke the ice everyone else joined in.

Whose job is thanking? Easy. It's yours.

If you are thinking that all this will take too much time away from your IMPORTANT work, I will again use my best counseling skills and encourage you to GET OVER IT. Remember, advocacy is important to the people and animals you are saving. Thanking is important to the people who are helping you do the saving. If done well, thanking is community development at its best.

If done well, thanking is community development at its best.

Another group of people to consider is your staff. Since these people are not getting rich saving condors from extinction, you presume that they are doing this work for love and they don't need retirement plans or decent filing cabinets. Think again.

And what about staff?

Advocacy groups that take care of issues but not the people who work on the issues are caught in a major contradiction of purpose, which they had better face. What does it say to an employee when you offer him disability insurance and an IRA?

97

It says that you believe he will be staying around for awhile and that you value his service to the organization. How about an improvement as simple as a comfortable place to take a break, with real coffee and tea? I believe that that tells your workers, paid or unpaid, that you are concerned about their burn-out level and encourage them to take care of themselves. And what happens when they take care of themselves? To put it bluntly, they last longer and give you better quality work.

And Then There's All of This Anger!

In 1976, I was the Health Educator with a community clinic in Santa Barbara, California. We were a collective, which means that once a week the doctor, nurses, therapists, receptionist and I would sit down to hash out every detail of running the clinic until we had reached consensus.

Santa Barbara is a beautiful seaside resort that shelters two classes of people: the very wealthy and the people who serve them. There are also students at the nearby University of California. The serving class are the maids in the hotels, the bartenders and cooks, hairdressers, contractors and architects, dentists, etc. Some make a living wage. Some do not. Freedom Community Clinic served those who did not.

Freedom Clinic's only real problem (besides trying to get rid of the crabs in the furniture) was money. We battled the state for family planning money. We battled the county for access to services for our patients. We tried to teach our gentle volunteers that asking for $5 from a patient for a physical exam was not ripping her off. We not only lived on subsistence wages in a very expensive town, but we went on unemployment every summer and kept on working to save the clinic money.

When the "Tax Revolution" hit California, it landed on organizations like Freedom Clinic. I remember the night Proposition 13 passed, cutting property taxes at the expense of social and other services. I could not believe people would be so callous as to pass such a measure. I stayed up all night watching the landslide returns, and I cried. Then I got mad.

When money became life-and-death for us, the collective at Freedom Clinic discovered another reality: politics. "Health Care is a Right, Not a Privilege!" we proclaimed righteously. "Do Not Victimize the Poor!" What kind of country is this that poor people stay locked in poverty because they keep having children they can't afford and the state will not give them the contraceptives they cannot afford! Outrage!

Speaking for myself, my anger could have filled four small countries. The life of Freedom Clinic became more important than the life of Burke Keegan. What was my small existence compared to the cause of affordable, competent health care? We worked longer hours, yelled louder, wrote more angry letters.

What do you do when you think that no one is listening to you? You speak louder. What if it looks like they still are not

I cried. Then I got mad.

listening? You might gesture to get their attention, or bang something. These techniques usually work. But what if yelling is your natural mode of communication? The first time someone hears you yell they might pay attention. But the tenth or fifteenth time that person encounters you, they will realize that yelling is the way you talk and will stop listening all over again.

Several years ago I was teaching a group of people how to ask for money. I videotaped them asking and played it back for the entire group. One man was a trial attorney. When it was his turn to ask, instead of raising his voice he lowered it until it was nearly imperceptible. He was smiling, his lips were moving, and when the group watched the tape, an amazing thing happened. Although they had seen several tapes before this one, they suddenly paid intense attention. They frowned and sat forward, trying to catch his words. They wanted to hear him. So when he raised his voice to ask for the money, his words were clear, his voice confident, and he had everyone's undivided attention. Great technique!

When the group watched the tape, an amazing thing happened.

...they wanted to hear him

In 1977, after worrying myself sick about money, and falling in love with fundraising in the process, I burned out on health education. Freedom Clinic, at this writing thirteen years later, has merged with another Clinic and continues providing low cost health care to the service class of Santa Barbara. I remain in love with both fundraising and advocacy, but have learned to take much better care of myself in the process.

The point of this march down memory lane is to share with you my conviction that taking a stance is an important part of life. But digging in your heels, forcing people to listen to you yell, whipping them in the face with your banners on every possible occasion, and putting your needs and the needs of your staff and volunteers last on a list headed by your cause is not your only option. If you choose the above as your modus operandi, consider the following:

❖ Burn-out. If the light of your issue is fueled by the bodies of burned out former workers, you just may run out of fuel.

❖ Sometimes yelling works. Sometimes it doesn't. Just for fun, try whispering, laughing, singing, cajoling, begging and groveling.

❖ You are responsible **to** your issue, not **for** it. Organizing is rewarding. So are traveling, sports, knitting, and watching soap operas.

❖ Think of yourself as a seed of energy for your cause. Take care of that seed. Water it. Talk to it. Give it light and air. It will live, and work, much longer if you do.

Fundraising for Advocacy Work

Sometimes it seems like the arts have it made. When they find a hot prospect, they invite him or her to a performance or opening. They take the prospect backstage... a little champagne, a little grease paint and the check is written.

You are responsible to your issue, not for it.

...a little champagne, a little greasepaint

Advocacy groups have filing cabinets and news clippings to show prospective donors. Although the volunteers in the inflatable rafts thumbing their noses at the whaling ships and saving those mammoth creatures are exciting, it really is only one whale at a time, and the strategy doesn't always work. And a lobbying group might fight for years for legislation only to have it overturned in the blink of an eye. And there are the folks whose issues are not even tangible enough to grasp: rights for the mentally ill, shelter for illegal aliens fleeing unimaginable oppression, end to invisible abuse of the elderly. What do these groups get to show the people who might be willing to invest in their work if they could just understand and **see** it?

Answering that question is the challenge to fundraisers in advocacy work.

The one thing that advocates get to show most often is their passion. Believing that your long, hard hours of work will ultimately make a difference is a very convincing argument. And people really do give to people. Interestingly enough, volunteers seem to tell passionate stories better than paid staff. In traveling the country and teaching, when I ask, "What difference is your organization making in the world?" inevitably it is the volunteer who is able to spin a yarn about knocking on a legislator's door, arguing his case, and making a difference. Some paid staff cannot even figure out what I am asking. They can recite the numbers of clients they serve, the size of their budgets and the numbers of grants they've received. That is

...it really is only one whale at a time

Volunteers tell passionate stories better than staff.

102

because that is where their heads are all day, every day.

Try an exercise. Stop reading this page and get yourself a pen and some paper. Answer the question, "What difference is my organization making in the world?" Whose lives are being affected? You may in fact be putting a small bandaid on a very large wound, but what purpose does that bandaid serve? What does it mean to stop the bleeding a little?

Now take a step further and write down how this work is affecting **my** life, as though you were addressing someone who doesn't know you. What if you are working on affordable housing? My life has to do with paying my mortgage in Mill Valley. What does your work have to do with me? Are you trying to stop tuna fishers from slaughtering dolphins? Why should that concern me?

What does your work have to do with me?

Read back over what you wrote. Read it, if you can, as though you were a stranger reading it for the first time. Is the passion there? Give it to someone who knows little about your work. Does it move them? If so, you are on your way to being able to tell your story in such a way that a prospective donor will be able to "see" and "feel" it in much the same way that a theater-goer gets goose bumps during a performance and is moved to write a check.

Another problem being faced by fundraisers who work in advocacy is that your "results" are usually not quick and neat: "There! That species is saved!" You may get the child care issue resolved with legislation, then abortion rights are threatened. You turn your attention to abortion rights, and the legislation starts eroding on child care. On and on. Even if you find people who will sign on and ride through an issue with you, it is difficult to get people who passionately care about child care to care as much about abortion, or any two, three or four issues you are tackling at the same time. ACLU faces that problem every day. Some of the folks they defend on First Amendment rights issues are fairly despicable people and ACLU often winds up infuriating their donors.

ACLU often infuriates donors.

A further complication many advocacy groups face is that they are not tax-deductible because of their lobbying work. It is true that the tax deduction is important to some donors, so many lobbying groups have formed tax-deductible foundations to attract non-lobbying monies for direct service work. This is a great strategy for organizations that truly want to perform non-lobbying activities. But allow me to add a twist to this dilemma of non-deductible gifts. In my experience, most donors decide to make a gift, then consider the tax benefits. The rich have plenty of places to put their money to shelter it; they do not need to fund political work for tax reasons. Lobbying work is funded by individuals who are passionate about the issues being addressed. I urge advocacy groups to state your case with passion and ask that the donor become your partner by giving the money you need to change the world. No apologies for the lack of tax benefits.

Most donors decide to make a gift, then consider the tax benefits.

It is true that all of these facets of good fundraising take time to care for properly. If your advocacy group's response to this dilemma is to put the donors on the back burner and let them fend for themselves, keep giving or go away, you are making a very grave error in judgment. It is important to acknowledge that keeping donors interested in advocacy work is difficult. But donor care and management is a program of any advocacy group just as is the issue you are addressing. The donors are advocacy's partners, providing the "something of value" (money) to make "something of value" (advocacy) happen. Without donors, at best your work is diminished. At worst, it goes away. Whatever amount of time it takes to keep track of what your donors care about is worth it. Keep excellent records of where their own concerns lie, and keep them informed about milestones as you reach them. Call them up if you can. If not, develop single-issue-oriented newsletters. And realize that they do not have to swallow the entire menu to be counted as loyal supporters. It is perfectly acceptable if some donors like one part of what you do but not the others.

A grave mistake made by all non-profits is insisting that donors fit into our convenient mold. They should just send money and leave us to do our work! The most important leap any organization can make in fundraising is to acknowledge that "our work" includes building a base of satisfied donors. It takes a great deal of time to listen to them, keep track of them, ask them appropriately for money and thank them **exquisitely**. Make the time.

Let us look for a moment at the circles in which advocacy

...I pulled off what I thought was the coup of the year. I enlisted a friend to get Jane Fonda not only to come to our dinner but pay for her own ticket and agree to speak. I went to my fundraising committee feeling I had pulled off a major victory. They responded by saying, "We can't allow her to come to our dinner. She's too radical." I was thinking of her as movie star Jane; they were thinking of Saigon. They thought every big Republican donor would walk out the door. It is the only time in my entire career that I planted my feet and said, "Either she comes, or I walk out of here." They relented, but then my real terror began because then the whole thing was on my shoulders. But I got to meet her limousine and be her escort at the cocktail party. She sat at my table at dinner, and was the great hit of the evening – conservatives and liberals alike.

groups move, and how these associations work.   People involved in advocacy work tend to talk to people who agree with them. They meet in conventions of like-minded folks and make speeches to each other. They strategize behind closed doors, and carry out their plans in secret. Given the way that the media is structured in this country, advocacy groups make the news, thereby reaching people who do not agree with them, when they either come up with a very bizarre strategy (ACLU defending the Nazis or NOW calling for a Women's Political Party), or when they fight with each other. The bottom line is that advocacy groups cannot seem to present their best face to the people who do not agree with them, and start preaching to the un-converted. Their press underscores the popular notion: "There they go again!" when extreme issues hit the news.

Advocacy groups also tend to do their fundraising within the same closed circles. When a gay rights group wants to do a mailing they say, "Get the ACLU list." The advocacy lists circle from one like-minded group to another, which means that those same sympathetic donors are constantly asked to save species, defend rights and pass legislation, while other potentially supportive people are never asked.

Talking to yourself has some real advantages: you know that you are being appreciated, you are obviously talking with someone who is highly intelligent, and you avoid both criticism and stupid questions. Asking only informed people to give means that, if they say no, it is because they're short of cash, not because they hate your guts.

...they do not have to swallow the whole menu

...thank them exquisitely

Talking to yourself has some real advantages.

106

The problem with talking to and fundraising from yourself is that the people who need to hear your entire argument, not the media-edited version, never do. If you are buying what I am saying about widening your understanding of "community", you will see that it is your obligation to bring the uninformed into your camp. The only way I know of to do that is to open up the process. Find the people who will at least listen and talk to them. Some ideas for how to do this are:

❖ Hold a special event that has some real general appeal (Bike-a-thon, House Tour, Concert, etc.) and make sure that everyone goes home with an informative, easy to read, short booklet.

❖ Try mailing to absolutely untried lists: small, obscure magazines, catalogue shoppers, people who have signed petitions. Just make sure that you think about who those particular people are and key your argument to their values. So, if you get a list of people who read mystery magazines, talk about the "mystery" of the environment. Or send catalogue shoppers a catalogue of ways to support you.

❖ Get into classrooms with your message, whether it's high school civics, college pre-law or local adult education.

❖ Place "human interest" articles in the local newspapers about your hard-working volunteers. And make sure that you get your volunteers nominated for awards when the community volunteer association asks for nominations. If they don't, why not start a volunteer awards luncheon for your entire community? Honor the woman who raised money for the town's Christmas toys campaign, the man who single-handedly saved twenty-three oil-soaked sea gulls, and while

How To Lose Donors Like Crazy

Tip #11: *Always use the salutation "Dear Friend" when corresponding with major donors. To sign the letter, use a stamp with the signature of the person who was President two years ago. Press the stamp to the paper, sliding it downward.*

you're at it, tell the stories of **your** best volunteers as well.

❖ Join the Chamber of Commerce and the most active service clubs in town. Stand proudly at each meeting and say who you are, what your organization is and does, and be sure to volunteer for the most active, visible committees. Also, make yourself available for politically-appointed commissions, like the Maternal Child Adolescent Health Board, or the Human Rights Commission. Working side-by-side with people who don't understand your cause is one of the best ways I know to gain their trust and respect.

❖ Encourage your friends and donors to send you names of people who might like to hear about the work you are doing. Make sure that the list of names includes one or two phrases for each name indicating that person's field of interest so that you can keep them informed appropriately.

Organizations run by minorities for minorities have some of the same problems, only compounded by racism. I have found it very difficult to convince minority-run organizations that they must stop talking to themselves and widen their listener pool if they intend to raise money and consciousness. But it is as essential for minority advocates, whether you are working in health care, day care, or in the arts, as it is for political advocacy groups to make yourselves heard in the widest circles possible. Do not presume that racism will keep everyone from hearing your message. Please know that there are some people out there who are not obviously sympathetic but who would be if they heard your story. I suggest that you try some of the strategies

Do not presume that racism will keep everyone from hearing your message.

listed above for opening up your circle and educating the community about the role you play.

We are seeing some dramatic education going on in minority communities around the issue of AIDS and being a minority gay man. At first, money was not flowing for minorities with AIDS because minority communities would not believe that there were gay men who were Black, Hispanic or Asian: "Not in MY neighborhood!" But as AIDS hit community after community, being gay was difficult to hide. Although certainly not the preferred way to come out, AIDS forced minority **and** white communities to identify with AIDS and face the fact that AIDS crosses all boundaries: sexual preference and race included. But before that realization could happen, minority gay groups had to do a great deal of education in non-gay sectors about minorities and homosexuality. Can you imagine a project more intimidating for the majority culture? I am sure that if it were not for the life and death circumstances they were facing, minority gay groups would have stayed in the closet and the truth would not have been spoken. The myth that all gay men are white and live in distant urban settings would persist.

A slightly new twist to "Not in my neighborhood!"

CHAPTER FIVE
Getting Jump-Started

The Myth of Competition

Competition is a very misunderstood concept for all non-profits because it is such a slippery devil. Let's take it apart and look at all of the pieces:

Taking Audience and Clients Out of the Equation

In the arts there is fierce, and rightful, competition for audience. Arts groups are not only competing with each other for audience, they are competing with VCR's, sporting events, movies, school functions, and everything demanding attention in peoples' lives. When "going after" audience, arts organizations must be willing to market aggressively and demonstrate why they are good enough for people to come see or hear.

...separating "audience" from "community"

If they are good, get the word out, and provide the kinds of art the community wants and needs, the audience is there. Once again it is important to separate the concept of "audience" from that of "community". The audience is the body of people who come to a performance, see a show in a museum, listen to a radio broadcast, etc. The community is the point of reference: the neighbors and donors, political and social contexts in which arts organizations make their art happen.

In social services, there should be absolutely no competition for clients. If two homeless shelters are competing for people to sleep on their cots, or two clinics are competing for patients to receive free health screenings, it's time to sit down and talk. There is certainly enough need to keep everyone busy. It is imperative that social services keep track of the need in their own community and work together to split up the pie. If there are two identical services competing for clients, your two organizations must share resources to make sure that the services are the best they can be, and then identify what else needs to be done and work together to accomplish it. By the way, this sharing of resources is very attractive to all kinds of funders who are looking for efficient operations to invest in.

The Myth of the "Fixed Pot"

If you've been around non-profits for awhile, you'll recognize this one right away. This is the line we've been sold for years, with governments, especially the Feds, shaking their finger at us and reminding us that there is just so much to go around. But in fact, "just so much" is based on a system of priorities that has other items at the head of the list. This myth has left non-profit organizations to fight each other rather than fighting together to change national priorities, and that lack of coordination has helped land us in the situation we're in today: "social programs" as dirty words, relegated to dead last in the funding lineup.

...there should be no competition for clients

This is the line we've been sold for years.

But we are not just talking about government money here. The myth of the Fixed Pot is the handiest excuse that exists for standing back from fundraising: "But there are so many non-profits out there asking! How can we compete?" First, you must understand that the pot is not fixed. In an extensive survey conducted for the Rockefellers in 1987, 40% (!) of the people surveyed responded that they feel that they do not give enough. And CASE, the Council for the Advancement and Support of Education, surveyed alumni who had not given to their Alma Mater. CASE asked, "Why don't you give?" The majority responded, "Because we were not asked."

The Myth of the Purloined Donor

Competition has been used as an excuse for why fundraising has not worked, but it is a phantom. In order for competition to exist between non-profits for the philanthropic dollar, one must envision the prospect standing on a corner, holding up a twenty-dollar bill. Whoever gets to the prospect first, or uses the best pitch, or uses the right formula will get the money. Then both the donor and the non-profit walk away satisfied and all other non-profits are out of luck.

This, of course, is simply not true.

People who give to non-profits generally have a variety of issues they care about. Very few people give to just one issue. In the course of teaching non-profit fundraising all over the country, I have come many times upon the misconception that

The majority responded, "Because we were not asked."

Very few people give to just one issue.

most people give to their religious institution and to nothing else. But the Rockefeller Foundation found, in the same survey noted above, that if a person gives to a religious organization she or he is more likely to give to non-profits as well.

If you buy into the notion that non-profits are competing for donors, then you have to take a look at the concept of stealing donors and buy that one, too. How might a donor be stolen from another non-profit? What could one non-profit say to lure the donor away from the institution they support and start giving their pot of money to another? I envision the non-profit thief running off with a donor tucked under his trench-coated arm. If the only way to get donors is to lure them away, then the non-profit they support must be proven unworthy, right?

I envision the non-profit thief running off with a donor tucked under his trench-coated arm.

Wrong. The only reasons why donors stop giving to one non-profit are:
1) They lose their shirts in the stock market;
2) They lose confidence in the non-profit's ability to do what it did when they first invested; or
3) They are not appreciated.

You cannot do anything about #1. Number 2 is your main business.

You must keep doing what you do better and better, and let your donors know what a great job you are doing. And #3 deserves your intense attention. Thank your donors! All the

Thank your donors! All the time!

time! In ways that are personal, genuine, and appropriate. If you don't, they will go away.

The Myth of the "Magic Bullet"

Then there is the misconception that all of the good fundraising strategies are taken. This fairy tale has as its core the myth of the Book of Right Answers. Well, someone must have the Book, right? Otherwise why would fundraising be so EASY for some folks and so DIFFICULT for us? With this myth in mind, I conducted my own survey this year (for a local social services agency) on fundraising techniques in Marin County. I talked to fundraisers from a variety of organizations and discovered that the direct mail they do doesn't work very well, but they continue to use it; that although special events in this County are very expensive, everyone felt that there was plenty of room for a really good, inventive party; and that major gifts from individuals are simply untapped. Most important, there was a sense from every fundraiser I spoke with that several other excellent organizations had some fundraising luck or skill that they themselves lacked. Yet when I spoke with those "excellent" organizations, they expressed a frustration that fundraising just wasn't working well at all for them either.

The discouragement that I hear in peoples' voices when they talk about fundraising is not really a reflection of "competition". There is plenty of room for excellence in fundraising. The discouraging factor is how incredibly hard, time-consuming and

There is plenty of room for excellence in fundraising.

scary fundraising is. I encourage you not to hide behind "competition" to keep from having to develop and execute a great fundraising strategy. The outcome will be directly in proportion to the commitment of the organization —staff, Board and volunteers— to carry out the plan. With fundraising, you are looking for a serious commitment to the task at hand. Folks who offer to "get involved" but refuse to take action will be of moderate service to you.

Commitment is the key. The difference between "commitment" and "involvement" is the difference between eggs and bacon. The chicken is involved. The pig is committed.

When you start fundraising seriously, you get to stop trying to change the character of the cheap unconvinced. You get to go out and find people who understand "Value for Value". When I hear "We'll try," from a Board member I put a pencil down in front of him or her and challenge, "Try to pick that up." Of course, the pencil is lifted immediately. "But no," I remind them. "I didn't say 'Pick it up.' I said 'Try to pick it up.'" The words "we'll try" do not belong in fundraising. Do it or don't.

Beyond the Myths

Fundraising is about teaching people to write the name of a non-profit on a check, and feel good about it. Rather than focusing on "competition", getting in there and beating out another non-profit for the pot, I recommend that you consider working together to help the people in your community be more generous! Share prospects! Share fundraising ideas! Go into the community as a united front instead of as "competitors". If every battered women's shelter in Northern California, or anyplace else, did a yearly campaign together and shared the proceeds, it would be very difficult for someone who cares about women and children who are beaten to turn them down. The problems of such cooperation usually boil down to the fear that you will not get your equitable share of the proceeds. It would take some pre-campaign negotiating, but your efforts would show prospects that the cooperating **organizations** support each other and that prospects can, too.

Why People Give

Why do you write checks for non-profit organizations? Chances are that your reasons will pop up on this list:

believe in the cause
peer pressure
good for business
to give back for
  services received
change the world
fun - to come to an event
status, ego
recognition

feels good
to get - as with premiums for
  giving
tax deduction
build community
vicarious artistic pleasure
guilt
fear
to make a difference

117

And the list could go on and on. I want you to realize that all of these motives are valid. They are human motives. People feel the need and they write a check.

It is very important that you 1) recognize that all of these needs exist, and 2) not judge them. Of course, we would all be very happy if everyone gave money because they believe in us. It would be a relief to me because then I wouldn't have to write this book or teach fundraising. But the world is somewhat more complex than that. If someone feels guilty for having been a lousy parent and wants to give your Parent Education Classes a gift, you must remember:

❖ You are not creating the guilt. You are relieving it.
❖ Involving this person in your work by giving him the opportunity to write a check and make you happen is allowing him to take responsibility for solving a small part of the parenting dilemma. That is the beginning of healing.
❖ Guilt is just as human as fear or joy, no better, no worse.

I suggest that you take a marketing approach to the list of "why people give". Rather than be intimidated by it, or judge what you perceive to be the more negative motives harshly, think about the list as a list of human needs that you have the opportunity to meet. Along with the needs you are already meeting for shelter, art or health care, you have a chance to meet the needs of prospective donors by giving them the chance to give. So if you know that a certain person in the community is

> **How To Lose Donors Like Crazy**
>
> Tip #6: *Run stories of employees' vacations and births of babies, along with election of Board officers and long biographies in your xeroxed newsletter... Send three copies to each of your donors.*

looking for recognition, you will tailor your approach to that person to offer her the best opportunity you have to give and get recognition: her name on a wall, in the newspaper or program, or even on a special project serving the population she particularly cares about.

The best way to find out where people fit on the list of motives for giving is to ask and listen. Sometimes you can find out from the prospect him- or herself. I once visited a prospect to ask him to get involved in funding a shelter for homeless teenagers in Los Angeles. The Executive Director and I knew that the prospect had been a street kid who had made good. I believe he owned a manufacturing company. He was already a donor to our Center, but we wanted a very large, one-time capital gift. We thought we had his needs identified and we were giving him the opportunity of a lifetime to help kids just like him who were growing up in the tough streets. We made our most eloquent argument, and he responded by flying into a rage. He told us in no uncertain terms that he had lifted himself up by his boot straps. There were no hand-outs for him. Learning where it's safe to sleep and how to hustle money for your next meal is a great lesson and he wasn't about to deprive a kid of that learning experience. You may think that this is a story of rejection for us, but it isn't. In fact, we learned more about him and his values in that session than we could have discovered in months of research. We did not get the capital gift, but we were able in the years that followed to present scenarios to him that met his needs; he turned out to be a very generous donor to the parts of the program that dealt with community education

❖ *When raising money for public schools in San Francisco, one older man said that he and his family had been in a concentration camp, and that raising money for this kind of an organization was his way to give back.*

❖ *At a glitzy arts organization one woman reported that she is a major benefactor so that she has someplace to wear her clothes.*

❖ *Some people report that they give to the Big Diseases out of fear.*

about who street kids are, and he wound up serving as a role model for kids trying to lift themselves up and "make it" legitimately.

If you cannot talk with the prospect directly, the second-best strategy for finding out what he cares about is to talk with people who know him. This is called screening. In the above example, we did in fact know many people who knew that prospect, and they could have told us his views on "hand-outs". But we thought we had it nailed. Screening with people who know your prospects will save you a great deal of time and energy. As you might imagine, if you know why a particular person gives money, what his or her need is, and you can satisfy that need, you are much more likely to get the gift.

If you know why a particular person gives money, you are more likely to get the gift.

The Most Important "Why"

I left the most important motive off the list of "why people give" because I want to address it separately. That motive is BECAUSE THEY ARE ASKED. Just because the motive exists for the prospect, and we can actually satisfy her need by allowing her to give, that does not mean that the gift will be given. The operative activity here is THE ASK. The old chestnut of fundraising is still true: "The right person has to ASK the right person for the right amount at the right time." That's all there is. Special events, direct mail, phonathons and membership drives are all window dressing. The ASK is the heart of fundraising.

Special needs events, direct mail, phonathons and membership drives are all window dressing.

"The right person has to ask the right person for the right amount at the right time."

120

But What Do They Want?

What do people want in return for their gift? First and foremost, they want their need met. Then, you must give them:

1) The sense that their gift made a difference. Beyond the essential thank-you note or letter, please take the time to wrap up a campaign by telling the donors what their money will do. When you finish a membership drive, tell the donors -- by letter, in person if possible, or in a newsletter -- that the campaign was a success because of them and what you will use the money for. And remember, the money is NOT used to meet payroll and pay the light bill. Those accomplishments, payroll paid and lights lit, allow something human to happen: dance class for seniors, network meetings of mental health clients, prenatal classes for low income teenagers. It is the human part that you will proudly display, not the internal workings of those activities. My esteemed colleague, Susi Scribner, advises non-profit folks to write about their work describing the situation instead of the need. Writing about the "need" leads you to write about needing to meet payroll. Writing or talking about the "situation" forces you to describe what is happening for people.

2) Ongoing involvement. Make sure that you **communicate** with prospects, not just ask them for money. Ask your donors and prospects, once a year, to give appropriate amounts. Then thank them in proportion to their gift: post card for small gifts, letter for larger gifts, tokens for very large gifts (paperweights, lapel pins, framed art work, etc.) But you may not leave it at

> **How To Lose Donors Like Crazy**
>
> Tip #2: *Write to donors only when you want money.*

Tell them what you are doing. Invite them to see their money in action.

121

that. Write them when you do NOT want money. Tell them what you are doing. Invite them to your organization to see their money in action.

I heard a story years ago about a new Director of Development at a small college. As he walked around the campus familiarizing himself, he noticed that a building, several benches and a park area were named for the same man. He went back to his office and looked up the name, but there was no record, so he went to the phone book and called the man. The man was astonished. He said that he had made those gifts twenty years ago, had been thanked once for each and then never heard from the college again. Needless to say, it took some work for this new Director to gain back the respect of the donor.

We often hear about "cultivation" in fundraising. We know that prospects must be "cultivated" before they give. This is absolutely true. This usually means acquainting the prospect with the work of the organization, giving her or him financial statements, brochures, tours. Sometimes it means several meetings with the prospect before the gift is given.

The Stanford University Development Office reports that they make an average of seventeen contacts with the prospect before the major gift is secured. But I want you to know that the cultivation BEFORE the gift is given is a drop in the bucket compared to the cultivation that must happen AFTER the first gift is given. Once the first check is written, cultivation happens in earnest or your donors will drift away. Think about them.

122

Confession: Always look a gift horse in the mouth

I got a call from an attorney who wanted two tickets to the black tie dinner I was giving – $150 a pop. In exchange, she wanted to give us a Cadillac! The mitigating factors here are 1) this woman was very politically powerful; and 2) she was a major donor. So, I said yes, figuring I could sell the Cadillac. So I put notices in the paper, and up on the bulletin board. One of the staff members finally bought it for $200. Unfortunately, before we could get the title transferred, he racked up four tickets, crashed the car, and we had to have it towed. That donation ended up costing us four or five hundred dollars, in addition to the pricey tickets. I don't know if she enjoyed the dinner.

Talk to them. Give them information and inspiration. Even though it is a major amount of work, develop a magnificent newsletter that does some of this work for you. Have regular, fun Open Houses. Go out to them. The Women's Foundation follows up on new major donors by calling them and asking if one of their volunteers can visit to get feedback on the program. The volunteer goes out with a questionnaire that asks the donor's opinion on the Foundation's programs, fundraising and image. She listens, takes notes, thanks the donor and leaves. In addition to getting a good sense of how they're doing out there, they are getting in some incredibly valuable cultivation time. The donor is then thanked for her input and kept informed of how her ideas were put into action.

Roadblocks

The major obstacle to creating an effective, thoughtful, dynamic fundraising machine is, I keep hearing, TIME. When I conduct fundraising seminars and lay out my thoughts on the care and feeding of donors, inevitably one or two people throw their hands up in despair and complain that these theories are just lovely, but how can they change the world **and** have a fundraising system that works? There's just not enough time. My response is that you cannot afford **not** to spend the time to do it right. Giving fundraising ten minutes here and four hours there will lead to more frustration than it's worth because that will amount to four hours and ten minutes totally wasted. Fundraising as a reluctant afterthought never works. Period.

Fundraising as a reluctant afterthought never works.

In order to get past this roadblock, remember what my teacher Flo Green says about time: we were all given the same 24 hours. The issue isn't time. It's priorities. If you are constantly out of money, you can't sleep at night worrying about it, you're burning out staff and volunteers by nickel-and-diming every aspect of your program, it's time to look at how you are setting priorities for effective use of your time. If your list looks like this:

1) paper work
2) clients
3) networking
4) meetings
5) fundraising

It might, with some reshuffling, look like this:

1) fundraising
2) clients
3) networking
4) meetings
5) paper work

Or perhaps someone could temporarily take over a part of your other duties so that you can spend the time to go out, get the money and stabilize the program. Once your fundraising machine is functioning, you might even see that you have the money to hire someone else to be responsible for fundraising. Or, my goodness, you might even fall in love with getting those

The issue isn't time. It's priorities.

124

checks and decide to hire someone else to push the paper.

If you are responsible for fundraising, I recommend that you put on your fundraising blinders and get to work. Restructure your vision so that you focus on the goal of having enough money to get your work done with comfort. Move aside anyone or anything that stands in the way of that goal. If you take this approach, your own priorities will change, and you will see that fundraising will begin to be another program that your organization provides to the community.

Focus on the goal of having enough money to get your work done with comfort.

Whose Job Is It?

I know of an alarming number of non-profits that hire a Director of Development, or, even worse, shuffle job descriptions to "identify" the person who will now be in charge of fundraising within the organization, and then take a huge sigh of relief. There. That's taken care of. He or she will do all of the fundraising, and we're off the hook.

Wrong.

The Agreement

Fundraising cannot be done by one person no matter who that person is. One person can be in charge, organizing and motivating others, and in fact that is a superb set-up. But the ideal staffing for successful fundraising is, quite simply, everyone: Board, staff and community volunteers.

The ideal situation is called "Agreement to Fundraise". When I am called in to fix fundraising that is broken or has never gotten off the ground, it is usually not an issue of poorly organized files, nor is it a matter of having a faulty idea or plan. Most often the problem is not having the Agreement to Fundraise.

As I was explaining this concept to a class in Boston several years ago, one young woman got that ah-ha look on her face. It seems that her organization had hired her as their first Director of Development, but could not find room for her in their main offices, so they rented her an office...on the other side of town. She had no typewriter, and her telephone could receive but not make calls. They felt that they had made an incredible effort towards fundraising by hiring her. But without the Agreement, they tied her hands behind her back.

...one young woman got that "ah - ha" look

The Agreement to Fundraise means that everyone commits to doing their part. The Fundraising Plan is drafted by the person with the most experience in fundraising; it is hashed out with the staff and refined, and it is presented to the Board. The Board not only gets to refine it further, but it is their opportunity to find, one by one, where they "fit" in the plan and roll up their sleeves for the task. I say "opportunity" because it is the obligation of each and every Board member to bring their skills to the work of fundraising. It is not enough to "guide" or "give advice" when it comes time to create programs. In fact, if a Board approves a series of programs, including salaries of the

Everyone commits to doing their part.

126

people to make the programs happen, rent on the offices where the programs will be offered, and any of the other necessities involved in providing a service or program and does not identify where the money will come from to make it happen, they are not doing their job. I believe that such a Board deserves to be walked out to the middle of the freeway and left.

Using Consultants

Where does the Consultant fit in this family situation? I have seen many non-profits try to shoe-horn a Fundraising Consultant right into the middle of the fray.... "You mean that you don't go out and ask for the money?" One of the Big Diseases called me once to ask if I would do a Major Gifts campaign for them. I was agreeable, until I learned that they not only wanted me to bring my experience and expertise, but they expected me to provide the volunteer askers and the prospects! I inquired if they wanted me to spend the money for them as well. I gave the woman my best "I do not provide the fish. Rather I teach you how to use the pole and where to drop in your line so that you can fish for yourself in the future," explanation, but it was no use. She understood the dilemma she was in. But it turns out that their first Major Gifts campaign was conducted by a Board member who did it all on his own. When he left, he took his contacts with him. And every year since, she has struggled to recreate that process. Her Board refused to get involved in Major Gifts since they had the history of having the campaign laid on them.

...trying to shoe-horn a consultant into the middle of the fray

127

Good fundraising consultants do not raise money. Therefore, it is ridiculous to pay a consultant a percentage of what is raised. That means that the consultant is getting a cut of someone else's hard work. Good consultants charge a fee and walk you through the steps, teaching you how and why, helping you to answer the had questions, and often taking the heat from volunteers and Board members who are reluctant to get our there and raise money. Furthermore, I believe that good fundraising consultants are invisible. If I do my job well and everyone is motivated and feeling proud of the work they're doing, I get to say, "Good for you!" and mean it.

Board Development consultants can help you to restructure your Board by suggesting different ways to accomplish your goals. And they can help to focus you present Board on planning, identify the talent you will need on your Board based on the Plan, and even help deal with the problem of dead wood. Good Board Development consultants get to ride into town, tell it like it is, shake everyone up and leave. My friends at Marin Abused Women' Services fondly refer to this process as "Board Bombing". It is often exactly what a stuck Board needs.

Use consultants when you're frustrated and not being listened to. Use them if you are just getting started and want to set it up right. Use consultant trainers to get your fundraising train on the right track, put your team together and help them to get the information they need. Use a consultant as a mentor. And don't forget to consider consultants as volunteers and Board members. Many of us are happy to serve on a good Board or

Overheard:

"How much are we paying you to do this? – Board member who has, involuntarily, just been taught how to raise money

"Twenty thousand million dollars." – frustrated consultant to involuntary Board member

get involved as a community member in a well-focused membership drive.

The professional organization for Directors of Development and Consultants is the National Society of Fundraising Executives. The good news about this organization is that they have created some standards and are helping to raise the image of the profession. They make their members feel honored. The bad news is that they do not speak at all to the needs of grassroots organizations. They tend to appeal to the hospital and university three-piece-suit types, and their meetings are full of the work "million", which tends to run off the folks who are struggling with "hundreds".

WORD OF WARNING: Anyone can hang out a shingle. Always, always check the references of a consultant. That way you will not only get a good one, but also the right one for you.

Part II
Cause and Effect

CHAPTER SIX
Making Your Case

In order to attract donors from the community, it is essential that you learn how to talk about the work you do in human terms. For those poor souls who have survived by writing government grants, this learning process will be very difficult. The dialect you used in writing those grants and reporting to those agencies have absolutely nothing to do with the language I am talking about.

For example, a social service agency might tell the federal government:

"The outreach department provided two hundred units of service to indigent clients in March including apparel dispersement, dietary supplements, inter-neighborhood transportation for retired persons and health education instruction for the physically disabled. One hundred and four units of volunteer service were recorded."

Interesting, isn't it?

The dialect you've used has nothing to do with the language I am talking about.

But if you were sitting down with a potential major donor over lunch, you might say to her, "March was a very exciting month for us. We found out that K-Mart was discontinuing a brand of clothing because of a lawsuit with the manufacturer. They were prohibited from selling it, so we offered to take it off their hands. They were thrilled! But we had no idea what we were getting into. It actually took sixteen volunteers, their pickup trucks and station wagons and one whole Saturday afternoon to transport the clothing to the Community Center, and another ten volunteers to sort the clothing by size and lay it out on tables with signs so that people could figure out what it was. We had everything from underwear for kids to whole jogging outfits, and in every size imaginable.

"I wish you could have seen the faces of the people who showed up to get some of the clothing. I talked with an older woman who came in one of our Community Vans. She picked out a sweater and some woolen slacks for herself, and took one of the little dresses for her granddaughter. She said that her granddaughter would be thrilled, because she had never had a new dress of her own.

"We served sandwiches and coffee, and the volunteers and clients acted like they were in a Rodeo Drive shop munching canapes and sipping champagne. They really loved it! And we're going back to K-Mart for a corporate gift.

"We also gave our first class on 'Sexuality for People in Wheelchairs' at the Community Center. Twenty three people showed up! The people who taught the class were in wheelchairs themselves and for three straight hours they had people giggling and asking really good questions. I got a note from one of the participants who said that while he was too embarrassed to ask any questions during the class, he wanted to know when we would present it again. He said that he had been paralyzed since birth and no one had ever talked about sex with him. He said he felt like a teenager again."

I am talking about presenting your case. The case is often perceived as a dry recitation of your mission and goals. It can be that if you are talking to someone who wants to know those things. But more likely your case will be a word picture of why you are important. It comes from your heart and leaves the listener or reader with a vivid picture of how you are affecting the lives of the people in your community.

Your case is a word picture of why you are important.

Writing a descriptive case statement is an exercise in creative writing. It involves being able to explain what your organization does for people, how you change their lives, what difference you are making in your community. You also must continually look at what your "case" is. If your arts organization hangs pretty pictures and has a nice garden to sit in, it is important that you get out into the gallery and the garden and talk to people. Why do they come there? What happens for them there? Are their lives stressed and this is their lunch time refuge? Does the garden remind them of their childhood? Are they art students who come to your gallery to be encouraged and inspired? Do people come and bring their children to teach

...what your organization does for people, how you change their lives, what difference you are making in the community

them the value of the arts?   Listen well, then go back and write down what they say.

If your lobbying group teaches grassroots folks how to knock on legislators' doors and talk about community needs, it is important that you be able to talk about why that is an important activity and about the folks themselves. Are they older women just now learning how to speak up for themselves? Are they young people who were previously discouraged about the legislative process but now feel like they are making a difference? Are they taking what you are teaching them and using that information to advocate for themselves in other parts of their lives? Are they having victories in affecting legislation?

I hear the phrase, "Tell your story!" said over and over by prospective donors to non-profit organizations. Please do not be so busy surviving that you forget to look at the tremendous good you are doing and learn how to articulate that.

Tell your story!

Writing Your Case

If you are starting a Capital Campaign, your case will be your justification for launching the campaign. Why is it needed? How will the project affect the lives of the people you serve? How will the project make your program better? What is happening in the lives of your clients that requires this project? How will the money be spent?

But don't these questions also all apply to your every-day needs as well?

Why wait for a capital campaign? Having several case statements on hand is like having a "photo album" of verbal snapshots you can show with pride.

...a photo album to show with pride

You can write a case for each aspect of your organization's work. If your organization is the Humane Society, of course you would have a case written on saving puppies. But you could also have a case on hand that explains the importance of your spaying and neutering program and what effect that program is having on the animal population in your community. You could have a case ready to explain how you can help people put the proper identification tags on their pets, including a great story about a "found" animal. If you wanted to involve the local vet school in volunteering and giving money, you could write a case on your volunteer vets that explains the benefits of volunteering with the Humane Society from the vet's point of view. **Each case is no more than a page long.**

Once you have your "photo album" complete, put the cases together in a binder and keep it close at hand because you will use your cases to:
> -thank donors
> -write feature articles for the local newspaper
> -train volunteer askers
> -write your newsletter
> -talk to major donor prospects

-write grants
-write direct mail appeals
-answer questions on a radio talk show
-give "warm fuzzy" reports at Board meetings

Any time you need to "tell your story" the story will already be on paper, told with a beginning and end, waiting for you to pull it out of the binder or your memory and show it to the world.

When to Launch a Capital Campaign

A capital campaign is a time-limited, intensive effort to raise a specific amount of money for a special project. This kind of fundraising tends to drain an organization's resources at the same time that it energizes them with new possibilities. In general, there are too many capital campaigns. A great number of non-profits that do capital campaigns could, in fact, do without building a new building, or probably should have leased instead of bought that new fleet of vans. Many organizations finish an exhausting but successful capital campaign only to discover that they cannot afford to light or heat the new building, or put gas in the shiny new vans.

More than any other kind of fundraising, capital campaigns must begin with every single duck in a row. Before the first dollar is solicited, every question must be answered, every problem solved, and every key player must be lined up, trained, and 100% behind the entire process.

Do not make the mistake of trying to do a capital campaign without a feasibility study. Even if you think that, no matter what, you must proceed with the campaign, please take the time to survey the community. In addition to the "go/don't go" advice, you will find out so much about your organization and who in the community can help you. You will get all the clues you need to create an effective campaign.

WARNING: Do not become so distracted by the capital campaign that annual giving suffers! This is a major disaster for many non-profits. Train your solicitors to ask for the gift, and to remind the donor that the organization will be back for their annual gift as well.

I am often asked, "Don't donors like to give to bricks more than just to operating expenses?" It is true that some foundations give only to capital campaigns. But that is not a reason to do one! The above question has more to do with stating your case than it does with capital campaigns. I find that people are sometimes reluctant, sometimes unable, to say what it is that they do for the community. Asking for money for a building with X number of square feet, so many windows and a garden full of posies seems easy compared with having to justify your existence. The volunteer solicitors in a capital campaign go out with 8 x 10 glossies of the artist's rendering of the building, offering to put the donors' names on the bricks in gold..."right here!" as they point to the picture. That feels so solid. It seems like a very real reason to ask for money, as opposed to making payroll. Even if it were true and donors liked bricks more than operating monies, that does not mean that you should do a capital campaign. Just present your every-day program as solidly as you would a building plan. Take them a rendering of your program in words. Show them pictures of people you serve, give them before-and-after stories. Paint it real. Help them to see what it will look like after they give their gift. Then thank them so graciously that they feel as if their names **were** etched in gold.

Launch a capital campaign when you have a very pressing need for the thing you are raising money for, when your resources are ready to handle the strain, when the community is behind you. Conduct the campaign with humor and love.

CHAPTER SEVEN
How to Conduct a Feasibility Study

The term "feasibility study" sounds very formal and time-consuming. In fact, a feasibility study is a survey, which can be extremely simple, that you do in the community to save yourself time, money and grief. I recommend that you **always** do a feasibility study if you are thinking about trying a new fundraising strategy, if you are unsure of the fundraising plan and need to see if that assortment of activities will work, or if you have an old chestnut of a fundraiser and want to figure out how to change it to make it better.

Start with the what. What kind or kinds of fundraising do you want to do? Suppose you decide to conduct a corporate campaign, but you've never done one before and you are not sure that the businesses in your community would support such a thing. Rather than pull the volunteers together, create a packet, train them in how to approach a corporation, and possibly fall on your face, be embarrassed, and not raise any money you could test the idea out with a feasibility study. Decide when you think you'll want to do your campaign, how much money you will raise, how much you will ask each corporation to give, what the benefits will be for the corporate giver, and how many volunteers you will need to pull it off. Write all of that down.

Then identify the who. Who you survey is, in fact, the most important part of the feasibility study process. It is essential

...suppose you decide to conduct a corporate campaign, but you've never done one before

Rather than fall on your face, and not raise any money, you could test out the idea.

that you contact the people who can tell you whether or not your idea will work. This is not a survey you do with a clip board on a Saturday morning in front of Safeway. You are looking to identify the key people in your community who know both fundraising and your targeted prospects. For a small special event, you may survey only five people by phone on a Tuesday morning. For the corporate campaign you'll talk to ten or twelve people, and that will probably take you one or two afternoons. The largest feasibility study I've done to date was for a $5 million capital campaign, and I spoke with 72 people over a three month period.

So who knows whether or not fundraising will work in your community? Other fundraisers do. Politicians do because they have to do their own fundraising. For a corporate campaign, you would survey corporate givers and people who are successful raising corporate monies. For a special event, you would want to talk with the media and make sure that your idea would fly in your community. For a major gift or capital campaign, you must contact foundation executives, United Way and big donors. The key is to ask the people who know.

The vehicle for the feasibility study consists of a cover letter, a copy of the survey, a phone call or personal visit, and a follow-up thank-you letter.

The cover letter explains:
1) What service your organization provides for the community

This is not a survey you do with a clipboard in front of Safeway.

...the key is to ask people who know

2) The kind of fundraising you want to do

3) That this is **not** a request for money

4) That the advice of this person is essential to the success of the campaign

5) When you will call to survey them or to make an appointment to do so

In the cover letter, do not presume that the person you are addressing knows what your organization does. This is a good rule for all correspondence with the community: explain it one more time. **Briefly**. If the person is affiliated with your organization, such as a past Board member, you may want to begin that paragraph with, "As you know..." But this paragraph is important because unless the feasee knows something about you, she or he cannot possibly give an opinion about whether or not your fundraising will work. If you want to do a $500 per plate Black Tie Dinner, the advice from the feasee would be colored by whether or not you are new in the community, whether or not you already have a glamorous following, and whether or not there are already too many Black Tie soirées in town. So explain what you do and where you stand in terms of the type of fundraising you want to do.

The "what" should be explained with enough detail so that the feasee can understand exactly what kind of fundraising you want to do. But make sure that you leave the door open for change. If you say, "This is what we are all set to do," I would counter by responding, "Sounds like you've already made up

...are there already too many black tie soirées in town?

If you have your heart set, save this step and learn the hard way.

your mind. Go for it." Your approach would be more successful if you presented your idea as, "This is what we think we might do. What do you think?" If you already have your heart set on the activity you're feasing, save yourself this step and go ahead and learn the hard way. Also avoid asking, "What kind of fundraising do you think we should be doing?" In my experience, the people you are surveying will respond with, "You're the expert, not me." So the "what" must have enough substance to allow the feasee to give input.

I have found it essential to tell the feasee in the cover letter that THIS IS NOT A REQUEST FOR MONEY because we non-profits have trained the community well that a letter from us means we want money. And be very careful here: This **is not** a request for money. It is a request for **advice.** The lovely by-product of a feasibility study is the opportunity to give influential people in the community some buy-in to your fundraising activity. If they helped to create it, they feel more connected to it. Remember that the advice of the people you are surveying is essential. I guarantee that once you've done a feasibility study and listened to the advice that comes back, you will never do a new fundraising activity without feasing it first.

If they helped create it, they feel more connected to it.

If you are considering conducting a large feasibility study, I recommend that you send the letters out in waves of eight or ten at a time, telling the feasees that you will call "next week". That way you will not be overwhelmed with the task at hand, you can add to your feasee list as new names come up, and you can balance the telephone interviews with the in-person interviews.

A face-to-face interview will yield more intimate information.

142

With a very large survey like my 72-person one, you will find that there are fifteen or twenty people who should be met with in person because they are very important in the community and very busy, and a face-to-face interview will yield more intimate information.

Smaller surveys can be done on the telephone in a fairly short period of time, so in the cover letter you can say, "I will call you next week to talk with you about this fundraising activity. The survey will take no more than fifteen minutes to complete." For a very informal survey, you can even skip the cover letter phase and call up five trusted experts in the field, tell them what you have in mind and find out what they think of the idea.

The survey is often the intimidating part, especially for those of us who studied surveying in college: analyzing the data and compiling the results. If you studied surveying in college, please know that this is a totally different animal. The survey, in this instance, is a list of questions you ask to find out if your idea will work. The more straightforward the questions, the more reliable the answers.

...the more straightforward the questions, the more reliable the answers

Let's go back to our corporate campaign example. Suppose the "what" of it is a six-week campaign involving ten volunteers who are all middle level managers in your community. Each will contact a total of ten CEO's for a total of one hundred prospects. Of that, you are expecting a 20% response, or 20 yeses, at $1500 per yes for a total of $30,000. You think it would be neat to then have those 20 corporate sponsors come out to some kind of thank-you luncheon where they see a video of your program and get thanked by the mayor.

The "who" of this feasibility study would have to include corporate givers, the United Way, and successful corporate fundraisers. The questions would look something like this:

1) Before today, had you heard of our organization? If so, what did you know about it?

2) Do you think that we can raise $30,000 from the corporations and businesses in this community? If yes, why? If no, why not?

3) Which corporations or businesses give?

4) Is 100 prospects reasonable? If not, what is a more reasonable number?

5) Do you think we can expect an average gift of $1500? If no, what is a more reasonable number?

6) What do you think the corporations and businesses in this community want in return for their philanthropic dollar?

7) If you are affiliated with a corporation or business, do you think that your business would give if approached in this campaign?

8) Are middle level managers the right askers?

144

9) Is six weeks enough time to make ten calls?

10) Who else should we talk to before we launch this campaign?

11) What advice do you have for us?

Type up the questions **single spaced** so that the feasee is not tempted to respond by mail. I have found that people who dash off a response by mail are usually negative about the activity and very terse with their advice. It is essential with a feasibility study that you talk with the feasees over the telephone or in person. You will find that they will give you some great ideas if you engage them in a conversation about your project and give them time to think of what would work best for you. The cover letter and the copy of the questions you will be asking go off in the mail to the feasees and you follow up by phone, either asking your questions by phone or in person and taking notes. I recommend that you type up and copy off some forms for yourself with the questions followed by boxes to check for the answers you anticipate and room to write down anything else of special interest that they say. That will save you some writer's cramp and ink. It also helps you look organized.

In our hypothetical example, I first asked what they know of your organization because their impressions will color their response. You do indeed want to talk with people who know fundraising, whether they like your organization or not. But in evaluating the responses, it is important to know who likes you and who wishes you dead.

trusted advisors, who assured me it was the worst idea they'd ever heard. I've still never done a community breakfast: anybody out there interested?

So suppose that everyone you survey thinks that $30,000 is do-able, that $1500 is within reason, but that six weeks is too short of a time and that you can succeed only if you have CEO's asking CEO's; middle level managers will not work at all. You look at the responses and gulp. You don't have any CEO's! You have three choices: 1) Say "what do they know" and go ahead with your middle level manager volunteers; 2) Throw up your hands in despair and scrap the whole thing; or 3) Put the activity on hold until you have ten CEO's lined up. Number one will bring you heartbreak because you will fail. Number two will demoralize you as you survey the financial hole you are still wallowing in. And number three will mean that you will have to put up with the financial crisis for awhile longer, that you will have to go up against your Board and insist that they get out there and find some CEO's, that you will have to put up with the demands and personalities of the most powerful women and men in your community, but it will ultimately mean success. It's up to you.

Once you have contacted all of your feasees and amassed the answers, compile and evaluate them. With five or ten respondents, that will be very easy. With fifty or sixty, it will take some time. Look for common themes and advice. When I compiled my survey for the $5 million campaign, probably 75% of the feasees said that the organization was virtually unknown to them; their advice was, "Tell your story." In fact, so many people used just those words that I became a little paranoid that they had gotten together to spook the consultant. But you will see that common threads and notions will emerge and will lead

You look up at the responses and gulp. You have three choices.

Common threads and notions will emerge.

you to some good, solid conclusions.

It is essential that you, as the person conducting the survey, follow some very important rules in reporting your findings:

1) Be totally objective. If you cannot possibly be objective, consider hiring an outside consultant to conduct the survey and to report his or her findings.

2) When asking the questions, do not lead the feasee by laughing or scowling. Just ask the questions and write down the responses.

3) Offer the feasee confidentiality. Tell the people you are questioning that you will report back **what** they say but **not who** said it. Then stick by that promise. I guarantee that your responses will be more usable than if the feasee thinks that his or her name will be linked to the opinion.

The final step in conducting a successful feasibility study is the follow up letter to the feasees telling them what you discovered and thanking them for being a part of the survey. With every survey I do, I write special notes at the end of the form letter pointing out that their input on a particular part of the fundraising idea was heard and included as a recommendation in my final report. So, for the large capital campaign, I wrote a special note to the mayor saying that her input on the plans for the school were heard, I highlighted her advice in my final report, and the Board of the organization voted to follow her advice to the letter.

Write special notes at the end of the form letter.

Many years ago I worked with a coalition of day care centers to coordinate a large special event. They took a class with me and came up with a great special event idea: conduct yacht tours in the Sausalito harbor! We started with a feasibility study.

The "what" of that event was fairly ambitious. They wanted to have a large party on the Sausalito waterfront with wine-tasting, a no-host bar, seafood tasting provided by 25 of the best restaurants in Marin, an art show, a poster for sale, entertainment, and tours of the yachts in the harbor. We identified eighteen people who we needed to survey: successful Marin special event fundraisers, Marin's favorite columnist, Beth Ashley, a political fundraising consultant, the local yacht club, some yacht owners, and some known Marin party-goers. We found out exactly what we needed to know to create the event:

❖ The yachts are not **in** Sausalito harbor on a Saturday in the summer. They're at sea!

❖ You cannot get insurance to do any kind of event with yachts. One scratch and the yacht is laid up for ten or fifteen days while the teak is hand-sanded and hand-varnished layer by layer.

❖ People were more interested in seeing the mysterious houseboats than yachts.

❖ People would pay $25 for such an event

❖ No one would buy a poster

❖ No one would attend this event if they just read about it in the paper

We found out exactly what we needed to know.

148

- ❖ No one would attend this event if they just got an invitation in the mail
- ❖ Everyone would attend this event if a friend invited them to go along

We took the results of our feasibility study to the houseboat community. In need of some positive PR, they agreed to cooperate. One feasee had suggested The Bay Model would be a perfect site (indoor/outdoor, large and free) and after one look we heartily agreed. We scrapped the printing of both invitations and posters, thus saving a ton of money. We put together a "committee of friends" to go out and sell tickets to **their** friends.

A positive side benefit to every feasibility study is the interest generated in the community for the event before it ever happens. The very influential people we surveyed thought that we were extremely smart to figure out the details before we launched a half-baked idea, and they were pleased to contribute to our thinking. The thank-you letter included the date of our brand-new "Waterfront Showcase" and a special invitation for the feasees to attend. After all, they created the blueprint for the party.

They thought we were extremely smart to figure out the details before we launched a half-baked idea, and they were pleased to contribute.

CHAPTER EIGHT
Unifying Your Theme for Fundraising

Try choosing a theme and doing all of your fundraising and marketing around it. Some of it will appeal to your current donors, but the main points are to appeal to a larger audience and to become identified with something of cultural or humorous interest outside of your daily struggle. You can choose a theme and do fundraising that applies directly to the theme, or that just mentions or suggests it.

Let's start with the idea of a Book Fair. Choose a theme: science fiction, cook books, travel books, whatever, that will help you make a name for yourself.

How to Start

Suppose you are The Marine Mammal Center. Right now what you do is rescue sea lions with injured flippers and sea gulls with oil on their feathers. And suppose that you choose to run a mammoth science fiction book sale. It just so happens that some science fiction writers are focusing on "pre-sentient" beings: dolphins and chimpanzees. Is there a connection?

You bet there is. Dolphins are sexy and beautiful, and your organization is on the front line of studying and saving them. Put dolphins up front: put them on your letterhead, talk about dolphin intelligence and research in your direct mail appeals to

...something of cultural or humourous interest outside your daily struggle

...science fiction writers and "pre-sentient" beings: what's your connection?

Sierra Club members and *Omni* readers, give an event that features a science fiction writer, sell t-shirts with dolphins on them. Your newsletter and other donor materials might feature comments on ocean farming, mammal research and other futuristic themes.

Why do this? In addition to being known for your work with sea lions and sea gulls, you will become known as a secondary source for information on "cutting edge" issues that are, indeed, in your future.

Ah, I hear those objections rising.

Bold image-creating schemes like this often never get off the ground because the Executive Director says, "Wait. We're more than dolphins. We can't put just dolphins out there. Find an image that represents everything we do." Such an argument is technically correct but reflects lack of understanding of what image is. The dolphin t-shirt will be purchased by people who think it's neat. They'll walk around like human billboards with the name of your organization on their chests, increasing name recognition and supporting your fundraising and public relations efforts. Eventually many of them will take the time to find out all you do, because your name is familiar.

Expanding your Theme

Starting again from a book fair concept, if you are an arts

...you will become a source for "cutting edge" information

*"Wait! Find an image that represents **everything** we do!"*

organization you can run a sale of movie books, posters and movie art through the decades. You can offer an event where MGM provides the costumes and make-up: say, a dinner dance where guests come in famous costumes and/or get made up (for an exorbitant fee). You can become the source for rare movie posters in their English or foreign versions.

If you have found a theme that appeals to many people in your area, regardless of your cause, there are many inherent opportunities to explore. Think about square dancing, gardening, antique cars, piano roll music, collectibles (counseling programs could feature depression glass), tatting, costumes, composting, dolls, sailboarding, iceskating, architecture, etc.

You really **can** choose a theme and build all your fundraising around it: direct mail, events, graphics, major gifts, promotion, marketing, the whole works. Sometimes it matters whether the theme applies to your organization and sometimes it does not.

Sometimes it matters whether the theme applies to your organization, but most often it does not.

So suppose you are the Museum of Science and Industry. You might choose robotics as your theme. You might have a robot on your letterhead. You might have a robot as an ambassador to the elementary schools. Whatever you choose, there will be magazines devoted to your theme. There will probably be fan clubs, booksellers newsletters, local public television shows, catalogs and any number of yet-untapped sources for reaching people through your theme.

...there will be fan clubs, newsletters, public television shows, catalogs and many more untapped vehicles for reaching people through your theme

No matter who you are, you could choose the mystery/detective

153

theme. You could do book sales, a murder mystery event, or have a mystery writer as a celebrity signer for your direct mail. In my town, anything to do with cooking — books, celebrity chefs, restaurant openings — would be a sure winner.

Depending on who and where you are, you could "do" wine. This means having a winery tour if you're in a wine-growing area; if you're not, you can still do wine tastings, give special wine dinners, invite wine critics or growers to a cocktail party or tasting. You could sell wine books, posters, or glasses; you could have signed bottles of important wines for sale. You could cooperate with local supermarkets (or specialty markets if you have them) to feature new products at your wine-tasting event. If you are a health care clinic in Texas (or anywhere else, for that matter), you could hold a Chili Cook-Off and Blood Pressure Clinic. Your letterhead could have chili peppers on it; you could sell cook books, posters, ready-made chili spices and cooking lessons. Whenever someone thinks of CHILI in your town, they'll think of you. And you become known for having a sense of humor to boot!

Three Most Important Things:

1) Find a unifying theme for your fundraising.
2) Have people identify you with the product and not with the fundraising need.
3) Stop being so damned serious!

In my town, anything to do with food is a sure winner.

You could become known for having a sense of humor.

How to Run a Book Fair

A Book Fair is an event where books of a particular genre are advertised and sold to people who care very deeply about that particular kind of book. It requires the choosing of a hot genre, the soliciting of the books and the organizing and sale of the books. This is not an activity that will make you very much money the first year. It will take some time to establish yourself as "The Place" to buy the kind of book you sell. But once your reputation is established, you can just take the money to the bank. Plus, you can build other events on this theme, as you will see.

What You Need to Start:

❖ Volunteers from the Board, staff and volunteer corps who are interested in the genre and who are willing to delve into their own personal libraries and approach their friends for the first sale.

❖ The first year, you need 500 books. Minimum. And four dedicated volunteers to schlepp them. And a dry place to store them.

❖ Begin at an established community event where you will try out your idea by setting up a booth. This could happen at your town's street fair, the Christmas Bazaar or the Community Picnic. You will find out if the community cares about this kind of book. Once you have 2000 books, you may set up your own event in a popular place (not at your organization on the outskirts of town next to the refinery). Choose a well-trafficked spot, do it every year, and soon it will be an institution.

Rules

❖ Do a small feasibility study to determine what kinds of books to feature. Survey all of your volunteers. You could even run the questionnaire in your newsletter. Ask what kinds of books they collect and who else they know who collects the same kinds of books, then assess the information numerically. Call everyone who responded and **their** contacts to see: 1) if they have books to donate, 2) if they know of books to be donated, 3) if they will come to the event.

❖ You will need to develop a relationship with local bookstores. Find out how they operate. Can you work a deal, for future years, with remainders? How can you cooperate, not compete, with used bookstores? Can you share with them, help bring them customers, help them get business through other events?

❖ In the meantime, go to the local bookstores and look up samples of the books you've selected. See how much they cost. You can add a little to the tab — after all, you're a non-profit — but you cannot price yourself out of the market.

❖ You need tough price-setters. Do not let non-experienced people set the prices. And do not lower the prices once they are set. EXCEPT...

❖ Allow your booth monitors to bargain just a bit on large sales: ten books or more. Your bigger customer needs to feel that she or he gets a good deal.

❖ NO TRADES. Sometimes, used bookstores will "trade" you one book for three, or some such. Sell each book or save it. Anything in your collection will sell, if not this time, then next. Your buyer is out there.

❖ Get the name and address of everyone who comes to your booth, whether or not they buy anything. They are interested! This is your mailing list for next year when your inventory is larger. Please do not put out a guest book. People **sign** them. You want people to **print** clearly their name and address so that you can invite them next year. Have a door prize. If you are offering mysteries, give a signed edition. If it's cook books, two free cooking lessons or a great soup pot.

❖ Serve coffee and punch. They'll browse.

❖ Have a secure money box and make sure that someone responsible keeps his or her eye on it at all times!

❖ Remember that this is where inventive, free and cheap advertising really works. Advertising will not sell tickets to your rubber chicken dinners, but it will bring in buyers for your travel books.

❖ Get your local elementary schools to advertise the event throughout the school and send flyers home with the students.

❖ Pay attention to local mystery fan newsletters or science fiction conventions as great opportunities for advertising.

❖ Do not let your volunteers buy up all of the books. This is not the idea. You are looking for new buyers... future buyers!

Twists

WONDERFUL IDEA! (pay attention!) MAKE THIS THE THEME OF YOUR ENTIRE FUNDRAISING PROGRAM FOR THE YEAR! (MAYBE FOREVER!)

❖ If you are an organization with transportation in your vision, like community vans for seniors and disabled people, take your show on the road. Do a Book van. Go to your Civic Center Farmer's Market, and hospital.

❖ If you are a free clinic, make your genre health care. Sell books, do cholesterol and high blood pressure checks, and throw in tarot card readings for the fun of it.

❖ If you are the local opera, sell art books. Have roving singers entertaining the crowd. Make it a medieval theme... sell roast pig, grog and baked potatoes.

❖ If you are an advocacy group, sell books by and about politicians. Get someone to make really silly buttons to give away. Make your door prize a one-week trip to Washington, DC; second prize, a two-week trip to Washington, DC.

The Three Most Important Things:

1) If you sell 75% of your books and have 75 people to invite for next year (the 75-75 rule), your event was a success.

2) The first event is a trial run. Put your money on The Second Annual. If next year you can have 2000 books and a celebrity to sign them, you are set.

3) The press must cover the First Annual. So make it newsworthy: Identify the key columnist and invite him or her as your guest; get the food editor to cover your cook book event, the travel editor for your travel books, science editor for science, etc.

CHAPTER NINE
How to Ask for Very Large Amounts of Money

First, understand that what you are about to do is unnatural for human beings. If sitting down with someone and saying, "And so, we want you to write a check for $10,000, what do you think?" were easy, everyone would be out there doing it and I would be slinging hash in New Jersey. So take a deep breath, remember that you are an important member of your community and that your organization is very worthy.

Actually, that's just where you'll start. Think about why your organization is so wonderful and worthy. What makes you excited about being a part of your organization? What is it about the program, clients, audience, Board, future that warms your belly and keeps you coming back? That is the beginning of fundraising. Attitude is everything.

Set a bottom limit for what you will consider "major". If you are regularly getting checks for $500, no problem, set the limit at $500. If a $500 check is greeted in your organization with champagne and feasting, then $500 is too high. Try $200.

The most important part of taking on a major gifts campaign is research. You must spend the time to do your homework. So start with what is called a Flat List. The Flat List is simply an alphabetical list of prospective major donors: people who can and might give you the amount you've set for qualifying them as a major donor.

What you are about to do is unnatural.

That is the beginning of fundraising. Attitude is everything.

...the Flat List: people who can and might give you the amount you've set

Where do the names come from? You will gather them from your own mailing list, looking for donors who responded to direct mail with an unusually large gift. You will collect ad books and programs from other organizations' events. The arts are especially good at telling the world who their major donors are. So are community foundations and large non-profits like hospitals and universities. Read the paper: society pages and the business news. Cut out articles about the 100 richest women in your county. Ask people! "Who do you know who could give us $500 or more?" They will tell you.

The Flat List is an organic document. It must keep growing and changing in order for it to be of real use to your organization. The best way to keep your Flat List alive is to screen it. Identify the people in your community who know who has the money: politicians, other fundraisers, popular philanthropists, people who sit on the Boards of major organizations, news reporters, columnists. They will be your screeners. Ask them to spend an hour with you looking at your list. This screening has some rules:

1) It always takes place in person.

2) Confidentiality is crucial. Assure the screener that you will not reveal what she tells you and ask the screener to keep secret the names on the list.

3) Do not tape record the meeting. People get very quiet when they are being taped. Take copious notes while the screener talks. You never know what will be of use later.

4) Have two sets of the Flat List: one for you to look at and one

...screening: you never know what will be of use later

160

for the screener. Both lists arrive and leave with you! Do not ever let the Flat List out of your possession. Letting the prospect names leak into the community will spell the end of your promising campaign.

5) Ask the following of the screener:

-Who on this list could give us $500 or more?
-How much should we ask for?
-What makes you think they might give to us?
-Who should do the ask?
-Who else should be on the list - who have we missed?
(Do not just gather names, get all the other information as well.)

6) In addition, find out who should **not** be on the list (just got divorced and is broke, never gives, hates your organization, etc.) and after you have heard the same piece of information from three screeners, remove that person from the list. You can do an unlimited number of screenings. The more input the better. After five or six screenings, you will find a few names rising to the top of the list as very likely prospects. It's time to buy some 3 x 5 cards and transfer the information to the cards.

I do not recommend using a computer for logging this personal information. You must be free to write everything that a screener tells you, including that the person is difficult, sick, cheap, lecherous, whatever. The cards are your personal record of the screenings you've done. You can share the pertinent information with whoever will do the ask if it is someone other than you. But the cards stay in your possession. (You can imagine what would happen if very confidential information got into the prospect's hands before you make the approach. Oops!) On the 3 x 5 card, make a note of who the screener is, the date, and write down everything of import.

In order for a major gifts campaign to work, one person must be in charge of the lists, the screenings and the assignment of the asks. It must be perfectly orchestrated so as not to appear to the community that your organization is running helter skelter asking every live body for a gift. You also must have at least three qualified askers. Each of your askers:

One person is in charge.

1) Must make a substantial donation first. This figure is not pre-set, but rather is based on how much that person can give. It should be one of the biggest gifts that person makes to a non-profit. From the writing of the check flows commitment.

Askers must GIVE, not be too terrified, and make a firm time commitment.

2) Must not be terrified of asking. People who are terrified tend to go out into the community and say, "You wouldn't want to write them a check, would you?" Fear, however, is okay.

3) Must make a time commitment to do at least three asks per month for three months (the 3-3 rule.) Anything less is not worth the time it will take you to get them trained.

Training, motivating and pushing are the key elements in making this campaign happen. Askers must be trained with humor and expertise, and they must be reminded of the seriousness of the task at hand. I recommend using a contract,

Training, motivating and pushing are the key elements.

or gentleperson's agreement, to sign the asker on and have them commit in writing to the job. Then the person who is chairing the campaign will assign the asks, based on the information on his 3 x 5 cards, and make arrangements to call the askers often.

Just a footnote: It is fine to set up the campaign with the askers going in pairs. This usually makes the askers a little less nervous, and while one is talking the other is listening and thinking. If possible, I recommend man-woman teams. Everyone relates better to either a man or a woman, and the prospect can choose who to connect with.

Going in pairs makes askers a little less nervous.

Another footnote: when you are out to lunch with a prospect, who pays? In a time-honored formula developed by this fundraiser over the years, here are the rules:

1) When the check comes, do not grab it. You will look like you're bribing the prospect.
2) If you hesitate and he or she does not make a fairly quick move either, reach for the check and be ready to pay.
3) If you take the check and the prospect says, "No, this is on me," hand over the check and say thank you.
4) If the prospect offers to split it with you, say "That's ok. This is on me." If he or she insists, say thank you.

...who pays?

In other words, follow the prospect's lead.

How to Produce a Black Tie Dinner

A Black Tie Dinner is a big-ticket, dress-up event where a great dinner is served and some kind of entertainment is presented.

You cannot do this unless: you already have enough donors at the big-ticket level to fill a room.

You must have a good drawing card. The event must be spectacular, bizarre or emotional enough to move wealthy people to put on a monkey suit or expensive evening gown and pay that kind of money for a banquet-style dinner. Here are some reasons why they might:

- ❖ Rule #1 concerning major donors is that THEY LOVE TO BE SEEN IN THE COMPANY OF MAJOR DONORS.
- ❖ Your issue is sexy right now.
- ❖ There are no other Black Tie Dinners in your community.
- ❖ You can tap into the "clique" that understands this genre.
- ❖ Your major donors need a place to wear their spectacular clothes and be seen.
- ❖ There is something very special happening at the event. Exotic food isn't enough. These folks can fly to Paris for dinner.
- ❖ They love you.

Before You Start You Need:

- ❖ A great site
- ❖ Twelve months lead time: it takes that long to book a good room. You're competing with weddings, anniversaries, bar mitzvahs, etc.
- ❖ A great graphic artist who will design spectacular invitations, the ad book, etc.
- ❖ Corporate/business underwriters
- ❖ A great plan. Morally, you must net more than 50%. But remember that this kind of fundraising is expensive. People who pay $250 want more than Chicken a l'Orange and a nice Chablis. Just be sure that it doesn't turn into a very expensive party for your Board members and their rich friends.
- ❖ To have a firm ticket policy. If the staff attends, it is acceptable to give them a reduced price ticket, but be sure that they have the appropriate clothes or they and everyone else will be embarrassed.

Twists:

❖ A color theme might work. The biggest event in San Francisco is "The Black and White Ball." For months before the party, stores are plastered with black and white evening gowns. It works beautifully to reinforce the event.

❖ An arts group in Marin County used to do the "Art and Garbage" gala, held in the local recycling center. The attendees really got into it. They wore corsages of dead cabbage leaves and ate their dinner out of tin cans, and paid dearly for the privilege!

❖ Do a Black Tie M*A*S*H Dinner. It's held in an army tent, food is served out of mess kits, and the wine is squirted out of I V bags. All of the sets and costumes are available for rent.

❖ During a Special Event Seminar I did many years ago, a Humane Society branch came up with "Full Moon Howl: Put on the Dog with the Humane Society." They wanted to put down a dance floor at the beach and have a Black Tie / Shoes Optional party: Luau food, dog-sitting, classical music. I do not believe it was ever done, but it's a great idea!

❖ If you have someone in your community who is beloved and has a great sense of humor, you could try a Roast format. This is a regular banquet, but the entertainment is a dias full of people who get up and tell terrible untruths about the person being roasted ("He's so cheap that...") You will need to hire a professional joke writer to pull it off.

"Important Things" check list:

❖ It must be a fantastic party: elegant and special with humor.

❖ The program may not drag on and on, so do not:

> a) allow your Board President to introduce every Board member in the audience and their niece from Dallas;
> b) give them every detail about your clinic or gallery. Put that information in the ad book or program.

❖ No staff skits! (Unless your staff used to work for Saturday Night Live.)

❖ No matter how innovative the menu, the food must be delicious and presented well. You might get away with serving chili, but it better be the best chili in the universe and presented with style and appeal.

❖ When your guests leave, they should be talking about what they'll wear next year and who else would love this event.

CHAPTER TEN
How to Use Direct Mail to Build a Community Base

FIRST, get a great list. DO NOT use the phone book, census tracts or lists of people who bought BMW's in your community last year. A great list has the following qualities:

1) You have reason to believe that the people on the list might like to know what you are doing, care about your cause, issue or art form, and might be moved to give money;
2) It is free, or nearly so.
3) It does not contain too many present donors or expired addresses.

In order to achieve #1 above, you must know something about the people on the list: where else they donate, or what magazines they subscribe to, or what their politics are. Just having money alone does not make him or her a good prospect. For example, an organization in Marin County that employed mentally ill and mentally retarded people as gardeners asked for and got the local subscription lists from a number of seed catalogs. They were given gratis (see #2 above). Two presumptions were made about this list: first, the subscribers were heavy-duty gardeners because they grew their plants from seeds; and second, they understood the meditative side effects of working in a garden. The letter was addressed "Dear Gifted Gardener" and the benefits of having troubled people employed in gardening were highlighted.

In addition to soliciting free lists, you have two other options: **rent or trade**. Renting is expensive, and sources usually specify that you can use the list only once. If this is the case, you can bank on the fact that there are "ringers" on the list. If a ringer receives a second unauthorized mailing from you, you will wind up in court. Also, if you rent a list, be sure to inquire how clean the list is (#3 above). Brokers vary widely in quality, with some keeping clean lists and some rarely verifying addresses. You could wind up with 30% or more undeliverable requests.

Trading means identifying an organization with a donor or membership base likely to be sympathetic to your issues and making a deal with that organization. Trading can happen openly or blindly. Open trading means just handing over your list. Blind trading means that you prepare 5000 pieces, sealed and ready to go, and the other organization attaches the labels and mails the pieces for you. Then you reciprocate. Whoever responds you each get to keep, but you never see each other's full list.

THEN, once the list is identified, you or a copywriter prepares the package. Very important: The letter and all accompanying materials are prepared with the prospect in mind. In the above example, flower seeds could have been included, sealed in a little plastic pouch, with "Free Seeds" noted on the outside. You already know that they care about such things, and such an enticement would surely get them to open the envelope. But "Dear Gifted Gardener" and "Free Seeds" would fall flat on the people who bought BMW's last year. Think about who the

*I was working with an organization that houses and feeds the homeless. We were talking about doing direct mail, acquiring some appropriate lists. I brought two personal observations to the task. Because I'm a fan of soap operas, taping them by day and watching them at night, I knew that my favorite soap was running a story on the homeless. I also knew that heavy-duty soap fans (like my mother) subscribe to **Soap Opera Digest**. So I talked the organization into letting me solicit the magazine's list. The marketing director for the parent company agreed to give me the list for free. I asked him if a non-profit had ever solicited the list and he said no, so it was uncharted territory. I asked for and got the list for Northern California. It was only about 2000 pieces, but the important part about this story is not the size of the list.*

people on the list are and direct the appeal right to what they care about.

The package should be attractive and readable. Use good colors - no institutional green! Arts organizations have to spend more money on direct mail, as well as all other printed materials, because you must reflect your taste and style. In general I recommend that the package reflect how much thought went into it, but that it never look like it cost a fortune because the prospect will think that you do not need his or her money. Design is all: you can go a long way with one-color printing if it has a great look. If the package is donated by the graphic artist, copywriter and/or printer, make sure to clearly acknowledge them in the piece.

"The package" includes the letter, a response device so donors can tell you about themselves and indicate the size of their gift, and a return envelope for the check or pledge. In addition, you might include a brochure, news clippings, flower seeds, ball point pen, button, or virtually anything to increase the likelihood that folks will open the envelope and respond. But remember, such enticements cost money and do not always impress potential donors.

THE LETTER is short and sweet. There are varying schools of thought on this, but I feel strongly that the people you are writing to are busy and non-profits do tend to go on and on about their need. Get to the point, say what you want, and get out.

The important part is that we knew several things about the people who subscribe to **Soap Opera Digest**. *One, if they watch soaps, they probably care about other peoples' human dramas. Two, if they read* **Soap Opera Digest** *they know the plots of all the soaps whether they watch "All My Children" or not. Three, it was a real advantage that the list had never been used before: we found people who were not always solicited.*

On the outside of the envelope, we wrote, "Guess what's happening in Pine Valley." We knew that this would make them open the envelope, which is the first hurdle. The letter was addressed, "Dear Soap Opera Fan" and the first paragraph was written like one from the magazine: " As Brooke searches for her mother..." Happily, I'd been monitoring this story, taking notes, and at one point Brook said, "I don't want to live in a community that doesn't

What you want is **money**, as in check or pledge. Say the amount. Say it several times: "Your twenty-five dollars will shelter a family for one night." "Send your twenty-five dollars today. Become a partner in ballet in this community." "Write a check for twenty-five dollars and sign on for the most rewarding partnership this community will ever offer you."

WARNING! Do not take your financial crisis out into the community. If you cannot meet payroll, you should not be attempting direct mail in the first place. Again, I am not suggesting that you hide your crisis or lie about it. If a donor makes an investment in you, he or she deserves to know the truth. But, "We have to have five thousand dollars to keep the doors open" is just not a good argument. They've heard our pleas for "Help!" too many times: Why are you cutting it so close anyway? Don't you know how to manage money? And if you can't run your organization like a business, why should I trust you with my twenty-five dollars?

If you decide to get involved with direct mail, you must be willing to present the emotional side of what you do. This is not an intellectual exercise. You must be able to explain why you are important, in human terms. What difference are you making in peoples' lives? How are you serving your community? And what are you offering to this donor: fame, glory, love, a place in heaven? This is your case: what is the situation and how can the donor get involved. Write about the people whose lives are affected because your organization exists.

care for its own homeless." Quoting Brooke, the letter went on to say that in Northern California we can be proud that an organization exists to take care of our homeless. There were four or five "bullets" describing the services offered, and a request for $25.

My favorite part was the P.S.: "Stand up with Brooke!" The mailing was a success in that it more than paid for itself and tapped a totally new resource for the organization.

THE RESPONSE DEVICE is your opportunity to collect some information on your donors. They are more likely to tell you where they work and what they do for a living as they are filling out the "donor application" than they might be at a later date. But make it simple! If possible, have their name and address pre-printed so they do not have to do that. Although you recommend a dollar amount in the text, have several suggested amounts printed on the return device with boxes to check.

THE RETURN ENVELOPE may be attached to the response device with a perforation for separating them, or a separate envelope, or they may actually be one piece. I recommend that you pay the postage for donors to return their money to you. The expensive way to do this is to stamp every envelope with a first class stamp. The less expensive is to secure a "Business Reply Permit" and send them this kind of envelope. You will pay only for the ones returned, but each piece will cost you significantly more than a first class stamp. A nice touch is a note on the reply envelope asking the donor to add a stamp, and save you the 35 cents, or whatever the going rate is at that time.

FINALLY, I urge you to try different ways to approach direct mail. Open all direct mail sent to you (and stop calling it junk mail!), keeping the good inventive pieces for future reference. One of my favorites was sent by Disability Services Matrix in Marin County. When you remove the letter from the envelope it has the left top corner chopped off. The first line reads, "We've cut every corner we can, and now we're coming to you." It breaks my law about not taking your financial crisis to the community, but I find that really catchy, effective direct mail breaks a few rules on the road to getting donors to write a check.

How to do a Phonathon

Asking for money over the telephone is called a phonathon; in newer parlance it is called telemarketing. Unless you accept Visa or Mastercard, asking for money over the telephone is, in fact, asking for a promise, or a pledge. When planning a phonathon, remember that that is Campaign One. Campaign Two is following up to collect.

For the sake of this discussion, we will segment asking by telephone into two distinct categories. Telemarketing we will consider being carried out by paid solicitors, usually hired and directed by an outside consulting firm, using a fairly large list. Phonathons, then, we will consider volunteer efforts to use the telephone to follow up on a smaller, in-house list mailing.

Telemarketing works best as a companion piece to direct mail. As a matter of fact, some of the really good direct mail firms also offer telemarketing services. So the mailing goes out to a somewhat warm list, which means a list about which you know some demographic information. Then a bank of trained solicitors calls the people who have not responded to ask them to give. The professionals tell us not to worry about making sure that only the non-givers are called. If someone who sent a check is called by mistake, it is a good opportunity for a human voice to say "Thank you." We also know that the letter must be followed up fairly quickly with a phone call because the prospect will forget not only the content of your beautiful letter, but will probably forget that he or she got the letter at all. I also found it interesting to learn from a marketing professional that the best time to do telemarketing is on a Sunday evening. People these days are out or busy on weekdays. Fridays and Saturdays are play days. Sunday evening everyone is getting back into the work mode, winding down, and ready to listen to a request.

The bad news about telemarketing is that the smooth solicitor is paid. I know that people care about whether or not the solicitor is paid, or getting a cut of the donation, because when I conduct phonathons the prospects ask my volunteers if they're paid. When they say no, the prospect relaxes a bit and listens. A few words on "paid" vs volunteer here. Calling and asking for money is hard work. It is honest work. People who do that kind of work deserve to be paid. But I do encourage you to resist paying a percentage to a telemarketing firm. If you know how many letters are going out and how many phone calls it will take to follow up on them, then negotiate a rate that still allows a donor's gift to make a difference to your organization. While direct mail and/or telemarketing can just break even the first few times out, I firmly believe that the lion's share should not be going to a for-profit "fundraising" firm. You do owe that much to your donors.

Very few volunteers enthusiastically come to phonathons ready to pick up that phone and get calling! Phonathons are, after all, just another strategy for having the right person ask the right person for the right amount at the right time. It is hard work. It can be scary to someone who has never done it before. It does take some practice. But I do find that volunteers who get into it make fabulous telephone solicitors. This is especially true of volunteers who have some kind of stake in the program they're soliciting for.

As with telemarketing, phonathons work best when they are a follow-up strategy to a mailing. My favorite phonathon is conducted by the Mill Valley Schools Community Foundation. They call their fundraising campaign "Apple Polishing", and they send out a very fancy several-color (donated, of course) mailing asking each family in the elementary and middle school district for $100 per schoolchild. Once the response to that request tapers off, we do four nights of calling using parent volunteers calling parent prospects. We do the campaign at the local TRI Realty office where there are plenty of phones. A local pizza parlor donates the pizza. Once the volunteers are assembled, we take 20 or 30 minutes to train them. The "script" is really just an outline because I firmly believe that a phonathon works best when the volunteer uses his or her own words. The outline looks like this:

1) **Identify** yourself: name, parent, volunteer.

2) **Ask** permission: "Do you have ten minutes to talk?" If not, agree upon a better time and make a note to call them back.

3) **Identify** the Foundation: did they get the packet? What do they think?

4) **Connect:** How does the work of the foundation affect your life? Think about it right now and connect in yourself with why the work the Foundation does is important to you. Once you can talk about that, you will bring life to your "ask".

5) **Ask:** Say $100 per child. But remember that our goal is 100% parent participation, so if $100 is too much...

6) **Negotiate:** Can he or she pledge half now and half later? Is a smaller amount acceptable? No matter what the outcome, thank them!

There are some twists to this campaign. We encourage Visa on the spot. And for $350 or more we invite them to a Major Donor party. Two years ago it was held on a party boat on the Bay. Last year it was at Bill Graham's house. Over the years we have found that people ask, "Where's the Major Donor party this year?" before they decide how much they'll give!

Training is absolutely essential. The trainer needs to help the volunteers understand the process and run through a list of Hard Questions with them, practicing the answers and reminding the volunteers that they do not have to be walking encyclopedias on the organization. It does help at a phonathon if someone is present who can field the more technical questions. Last year the Schools Foundation made a video tape of my training and made sure that there was a VCR on hand at the phonathon. That saved me having to go there four nights in a row as I had done for three or four years. And it meant that the folks who dribble in late can be sat down and trained with little effort.

Finally, remember that hardly anyone collects 100% of pledges. I've heard tell that the Jerry Lewis Telethon collects only 40%. The Schools Foundation collects more than 80%, but they certainly wish it were 100! I recommend, for the purposes of your phonathon, that you count all pledges on a "Pledge Tote Board" during the phonathon, and if you do it over several nights that you keep a running total. But for planning purposes, count only cash in hand and do not beat yourself up over uncollected pledges. Some organizations that handle many pledges of various sizes and with various due dates hire a billing firm to remind donors and keep track of payments. This is a very good alternative to taking pledges and devoting your precious time to chasing the cash.

CHAPTER ELEVEN
How to Conduct a Membership Drive

A Membership Drive is a volunteer-intensive effort to reach potential donors through direct personal contact. IT IS NOT A DIRECT MAIL CAMPAIGN, NOR IT IS A PHONATHON. The key to the success of a Membership Drive is signing up volunteers who will solicit their friends, families and co-workers in person, thereby reaching a large pool of people that you would not ordinarily reach. Face-to-face solicitation is the most effective way to raise money. It is also the cheapest.

Face-to-face solicitation is the most effective way to raise money.

Setting Your Goal

Start by setting a goal. Can you name 100 people who can raise $200 each for you? If that is impossible, can you name 100 people who can raise $100? If all of that is very easy, how about 200 people at $200? I have conducted Membership Drives that had 10 people raising $500 each, 50 people raising $250 each and 300 people raising $200 each. The process itself is totally adaptable to the reality of your volunteer base. Just be sure to judge your capabilities realistically. You want to reach your goal.

...adapt the process to the reality of your volunteer base

Recruiting and Training Volunteers

Once the goal is set, reach for your rolodex and start identifying those volunteers' names. Make a list of who you think will follow through, and then start calling them. When you call your volunteers to sign them up, it is absolutely essential that you tell them **everything** that is expected of them. The more realistic you can be with your expectations, the more likely they will be to either bow out if it is not for them, or sign on with full knowledge of what they will need to do.

So think through what you want from the volunteer, then write a job description. Requirements might include:

1) **Write a check.** It is very difficult to ask someone to do something that you yourself are not willing to do. The first dollar commitments should come from your fundraising volunteers.

2) **Meet their goal.** If you need a pyramid of 200 people raising $200 each to meet your goal of $40,000, then everyone has to commit to the goal of $200 to get there.

3) **Get trained.** Actually, this one is not negotiable. It is a true fundraiser's nightmare to turn 200 untrained volunteers loose on your town, each giving his or her version of what your organizations does! But if you want anyone to show up for training, be sure to call it something else..."Volunteer Welcome" or "Pre-Campaign Party". Make sure to keep them for no more than 90 minutes, give them a packet of information (see step #4), brainstorm with them who they think they'll ask so that others will get some new, good ideas for prospects, and give them an

*...tell them **everything** that is expected of them*

178

them an easy-to-remember explanation of what your organization does and why.

4) **Understand and use the packet of information** you give them at the "Party" to answer any questions that prospective donors might have. The packet might include a financial statement, brochures, membership applications, copies of news clippings, list of Board members, brief history, and anything else that seems relevant and will help them to answer questions.

5) **Attend the Kick-Off and Victory parties.** The Kick-Off happens after everyone is trained and the Campaign is ready to start. The Victory Party celebrates the end of the Campaign and the effort that was expended. The Victory Party happens even if you did not reach your goal!

6) **Attend Check-in Parties.** If your Campaign is longer than six weeks, you will need to gather the troops at least once every two weeks to re-energize them for the task at hand.

Meeting Your Goal

Membership Drives can last for up to six weeks, or be a short as 48 hours. When planning yours, remember that no matter how long or short the Drive is, everyone will complain that they didn't have enough time, and 60% of the money will come in during the last six minutes of the Campaign. In my experience, 2 weeks is plenty of time to raise up to $5000.

...no matter how long or short the Drive, 60% of the money will come in during the last six minutes

Volunteers can meet their goal any way they want — soliciting co-workers at the office, calling friends on the phone, writing notes to acquaintances and following up with a call, but one of the more enjoyable aspects of asking volunteers to sign on for a Membership Drive is telling them they can give a party to raise their money. It can be a party where their friends are invited to their home and told that there will be a pitch so they should bring their checkbooks. Or, better still, they can give a party just as usual, but charge everyone $25 or $30 to come; guests can drop their checks in a basket at the door and nothing else need be said. For populations of people who like to give parties, and do it often, this can be a wonderful and easy way to raise some money for their favorite cause. The only rule about parties during Membership Drives is that the volunteer host must always pick up the tab. Your organization cannot afford the money nor the negative publicity on throwing parties for your prospects. And every guest/donor must leave with a brochure or information sheet. They'll be hearing from your organization again!

Give a party!

The prizes should be solicited and the parties totally fleshed out with time, place and refreshments secured before you have your Kick-Off. You can work out these details as you are playing phone tag with your volunteers to ask them to do the soliciting.

Confession

The first Membership Drive I produced in 1980 involved 300

180

volunteers each raising $200. Here are the mistakes I made:

First, I was not firm enough when I signed them on. When a volunteer would ask, "What if I don't make my goal?" I would respond, "Oh, don't worry, you'll do fine." Consequently, many did not make their goal and the Campaign raised $43,000 instead of the hoped-for $60,000. If I had it to do over again, I would smile and say, "Raise it or write it."

I also became so depressed at falling short of my goal that I took to my bed, only to be rousted out by the Executive Director who reminded me that I had just RAISED $43,000!

Secondly, I scheduled two nights of training to give them a choice, and I called it TRAINING. I rented a hall, made the coffee, set up the chairs, and "trained" two nights of empty chairs. By Kick-Off Saturday, less than 1/3 of the volunteers were trained. I spent the entire Kick-Off training people on the hoof, and quite literally spent the rest of the Drive training people on the phone one at a time. The next year, when I called to sign people up, I told them that a pre-Campaign meeting with me was mandatory, and I would meet with them where and when they wanted. I scheduled them in groups as much as I could, but some of them I did one-on-one. It was a great deal of work before the Campaign began, but it saved a great deal of pain in the long run.

Third, I decided that the Campaigners should have baseball caps to wear at the Kick-Off. The theme that year was "Declare

Our Independence from Government Funding." Since our agency lost half of our staff and 1/3 of our budget to CETA VI cuts, we were going to take our lemons and make lemonade! We got a brass band, a parade permit, and invited the media to join our "celebration". Since every other non-profit in Los Angeles was screaming about the cuts, we were newsworthy! I had the assurances of every major news station that they would cover it. The photos of the Kick-Off show me either running along side someone trying to train them as we marched, or screaming through a bullhorn, "Put on your hats!" trying to get everyone to buy into my stupid idea. It would have been more effective to get a committee of volunteers to figure out how to get everyone trained, and what kind of hat/shirt/whatever they wanted to wear. By the way, all of my fashion coordination was for naught. That morning in Los Angeles a hostage was taken in a bank robbery and there went all of my news coverage!

"Put on your hats!"

Fourth, I held Check-In Parties at the second and fourth weeks of my six-week Campaign, when there was really very little to report. I counted every dime that came in, including our United Way designations and the last dribbles of the Christmas mailing. But it wasn't very inspiring until the gush at the very end. The next year I spent some of that very hectic pre-Campaign time to send a renewal mailing to everyone who had joined in the previous year's campaign. By the time we Kicked Off, I had raised $15,000 toward our $60,000 goal, but I didn't tell any of the Campaigners yet. At the first Check-In Party two weeks into the Campaign, I unveiled with great fanfare our thermometer—reading $15,000! Of course, no one in the room

They all exploded from the room, raring to catch up!

had raised a dime except me, but no one was about to say, "Wait a minute! I haven't raised a dime, have you?" Every volunteer thought they were the only shirkers, and the Campaign was taking off without them. They all exploded from the room, raring to catch up with this exciting Campaign!

Finally, what I learned from my first Campaign was the three C's: Call Campaigners Constantly. I was calling to make sure that they were comfortable with the material and to find out what they were hearing from the community. But the side effect was that my call kept them on their toes and reminded them to get out there and ask! The second year, I recruited a very popular and charismatic local minister to be Honorary Chair and gave him the job of calling all of my Campaigners once toward the end of the Campaign. It worked because of his excellent follow-through and great reputation in the community.

Call Campaigners Constantly.

Publicizing Your Drive

Public relations, or marketing, for a Membership Drive is **never** done to bring in donors. People get very confused about the value of PSA's and street banners: these strategies do not raise money. People raise money. Especially in a Membership Drive. The only reason to include PR in your Campaign is to keep the **volunteers** excited.

PSA's and street banners do not raise money. People raise money.

You may want to try putting together a PR team of volunteers who devise the strategy, including the theme of the Campaign, and do the writing and production of the PR materials. I worked with a wonderful man in Southern California who began volunteering with the organization by designing the logo. He then worked with me on other small projects, like silk screening flags (until 2 a.m.) and designing invitations. When it came time to do my first Membership Drive, I asked Bob to figure out how to get three street banners over the major streets where my volunteer fundraisers lived. I went off soliciting prizes and volunteers and gave the banners not one more thought. On the day of the Kick-Off parade, I arrived at the Center and there was the banner proclaiming "Declare Our Independence" stretched across the street. We all hear a great deal of complaining about how much time it takes to find and keep good volunteers. Just as with donors, I maintain that it is more than worth the effort.

The time it takes to find and keep good volunteers is more than worth the effort.

Public relations for a Membership Drive should serve to remind your volunteers that they are involved in a wonderful, exciting activity. Some strategies (in addition to street banners) that might work are:

❖ Campaign Newsletters. If your Campaign is more than ten days long, consider sending all of your volunteers a rah-rah Newsletter. You can actually lay out the Newsletter before the Campaign, complete with human interest stories about clients and volunteers, and great ideas for how to reach their goals, then plug in the pie charts and mail it.

❖ Conduct a quick survey before the Campaign begins to find out which radio stations your volunteers listen to regularly.

Dance with them!

Sift out the eight or ten most popular – this will be easier in smaller towns. When you send in your PSA to the targeted radio station, tell them in the cover letter that they were voted one of the most popular by the volunteer base you are trying to reach. Be sure to follow the rules for each radio station about length and quality of the PSA or it will not get aired.

❖ With smaller numbers of Campaigners, the "flower brigade" idea would work wonderfully. Early one morning about 2/3 through the Campaign, buy roses. Then send out your carefully orchestrated band of volunteers to put one rose with a ribbon and a thank-you note on either the door knob or windshield (if you know which car is theirs) of each Campaigner. There's not a soul I know who does not like getting flowers.

Finally, a few words about the Victory Party. This fun activity is your best opportunity to thank your volunteers. Make it open to volunteers and "significant others". It is acceptable to sell alcoholic drinks (unless you are a recovery center!) for a small price, but be sure to have food, sodas or coffee and entertainment for free. Give them praise! Give them prizes! Dance with them! Make them feel wonderful and appreciated.

This is the outline. I challenge you to take it and make it your own. It happens to be my favorite way to raise money. It is very cost-effective because of the use of volunteers. You just need to print thank-you letters and membership applications and pay to put all of those names in your computer. It is fun! In all of my years doing Membership Drives with various non-

I worked with an advocacy group that was stalled on their annual membership drive and wanted my help motivating their Board members and volunteers to get ready to do it again. When I explored the reasons for the inertia, I discovered that at the Victory Party the year before, the Chair of the Campaign got up and blasted the volunteer Campaigners for not meeting their goal. He recounted all of the work that would not get done that year because they had not worked hard enough. This was a very serious, dedicated group and they were clearly bummed out. We took a great chance and decided to jolt them out of their blues. We called the Sisters of Perpetual Indulgence, a San Francisco-based group of men who dress up like nuns and provide comic and satiric relief for just such occasions. I invited

profits, I've only had one person say, "That was an awful experience. Don't ever ask me to do that again." In fact, most of my Campaigners signed up at the Victory Party for next year's Drive!

You can give the basic structure any number of twists:

❖ I've always wanted to raise $72,000 in 72 hours. This would take more advance planning, but you still could line up your volunteers and have them create a Fundraising Weekend, with the Kick-Off on Thursday after work and the Victory Party and money turn-in on Sunday evening.

❖ Get kids to raise the money. Of course, it would be in smaller amounts, but a high school athletic team could sign up their friends and relatives at $5 each and raise a fair amount of money in two weeks.

❖ Use video tape to train your volunteers. You would have to be absolutely sure that they would really watch it, but with ten copies of a very high quality, funny tape, you would save an impressive amount of shoe leather. Perhaps you could run a contest to get the volunteers to identify six animal sounds incorporated throughout the tape and give a prize to the winners.

them to my campaign training. I started off very somber, talking about the seriousness of the fundraising effort, when two absolutely outrageous "nuns" burst through the door, yelling at me for being too serious. The volunteers had no idea what to do. "Sister Sadie" proceeded to inform them that "she" knew they had not met their goal the previous year, and passed out absolution cards, forgiving them of their sins during the previous Campaign. The laughter rippled, and then rolled through the room. I was very relieved that it had worked. But I encourage you to keep yourself out of that difficult spot by using the Victory Party to celebrate, even if the goal is not quite met.

CHAPTER TWELVE
Special Events

Good News/Bad News

Ah, special events. The first person who ever said, "My uncle has a barn, let's give a dance!" is probably in some special fundraisers' hell where the band is always two hours late, the volunteers eat all the canapés before the party starts, and there's a flash flood warning on the radio. On the other hand, there's often not enough attention paid to the need for celebration, affirmation and just plain silly fun in our oh-so-serious lives. A good special event can do wonders for your community image, can bring new energy and life to your organization, and can even make some money. A tacky event, or one that flops for reasons either within or beyond your control, can cost you many hard-won dollars, burn out your Board, staff and volunteers and, most significantly, discourage or even offend your major and minor donors. And hear this now: Special events are demonstrably the **least** efficient way to raise money.

So Why Do Them At All?

First, because done right, they are a lot of fun. A special event can be your "present" to the community: a time to put aside everyday worries, a time for those who love you to show their support. Special events can appeal to new audiences, people of

The first person who ever said, "My uncle has a barn, let's give a dance!" is probably in some special fundraisers' hell.

Special events are demonstrably the least efficient way to raise money.

different ages and interests than those who generally walk through your door or renew their annual membership. Events can raise community consciousness by highlighting a new or special part of your program and by being newsworthy in themselves. Events can lift morale and renew faith in your organization when you make exciting connections with other parts of the community. Special events can bring new faces into your "family" of donors, volunteers and potential Board members. Lastly, they can make money. However, please note right now that there are a zillion other ways to accomplish the above. Before you charge into event planning, make damn sure this is the way you want to go.

...new audiences, ages, interests

...new faces into your "family"

Events and Your Fundraising Plan

First off, study your fundraising plan. What place do events occupy in it? Should your emphasis be changed? Why? How much have you projected to spend and net on the event? Do you have a track record, and are your projections in line with it?

In general, you should never, ever, plan more than two events a year unless your organization covers so large a geographical community that you can pull off a moveable feast, or has a self-renewing and very large fundraising auxiliary. The auxiliary model is becoming rarer and rarer these days. It's a great model and we all mourn its passing, but it simply is not practical any more for most communities. What you do, of course, is create time-limited mini-auxiliaries for each of your special events.

Another fixed-group model we're seeing more of is the "service club" (including civic group, trade or professional organization, special interest or hobby group, and so on) sponsorship and even production of special events. Definitely, cultivate and nurture this model in your community: these groups are gold mines of new people to invite, have business connections beyond your wildest dreams and can help you achieve true community partnership in your work.

Getting back to your Fundraising Plan: Do events only as part of a diverse set of activities; know exactly why you are doing any event; set down clear goals in terms of participation, attendance, community relations, and dollar net. Never plan an event in an emergency — i.e., to keep your doors open. You won't have the time or energy to do it right, and I promise you it won't work out.

Never plan an event in an emergency. I promise you it won't work out.

Getting Help

It is always possible, of course, to "hire out" an event. There are firms specializing in various events — art auctions, fashion shows and gourmet food fairs are good examples. You hire them and they produce the event, soup to nuts, sometimes for a percentage of the gross, most often for a flat fee. This approach, obviously, can be wonderful in terms of saving staff and volunteer time and of getting the details done by experts. But I urge you to think extremely carefully about this before you leap: **1)** "Canned event" producers, although their events have wide

...it is still your responsibility to get folks there

appeal, cannot develop and will not guarantee your attendance; it is still your responsibility to get folks there; **2)** You may get confused responses from your guests when they discover you are paying "outsiders" a large percentage of the take (see: telemarketing); and **3)** You, and your organization, will not "own" the event in several very important ways. You will also hear about event producers who bring along their own audiences, sponsors and so on. Of course, this works. Once. Again, your costs may be pretty high . . . and what have you really gained?

It is often a perfectly reasonable idea to hire someone to help you, particularly if you are a first-time event producer or you have been charged with re-animating a washed-out, wrung-out party. Your goals in this should be to **1)** learn how to do it yourself; and **2)** help your whole organization grow to "own" the event. At Keegan Fundraising, we are often asked to coordinate special events, but we agree to it only if the organization wants to learn how to avoid hiring us back the following year. Over our umpty-odd combined years of special events, we've given parties that no one came to, events that were inappropriate, events that were just plain gruesome. We've also given events that really worked, really made money, and really were fun. So we've learned, and enjoy passing on every little bit. Having a teacher or "expert" can be helpful, especially if your Board needs direction and finds it hard to accept it from you. The rules are here for you, in this chapter. Sometimes you'll say, "Now, really, she's gone too far," but these are rules learned in the trenches from long, funny and

...I have great memories of working with the organization called Events Unlimited in LA which helped us invite people, coordinate with the hotel, get M&M's in Joel Grey's dressing room, etc. But my favorite memory is having my three fundraising committee members, two judges and an attorney, fussing over who sits where. Is the first balcony more prestigeous than the back of the main hall? Who gets to sit next to the kitchen? Who got drunk last year and this year needs to sit by the door?

Learn how to do it yourself.

...help your whole organization "own" the event

occasionally tragic experience. If you are considering getting help in, essentially, the form of a part-time staff member, find someone with a real track record — paid or unpaid — of great parties. This is no time to offer an internship. Check references thoroughly, and make sure that you are hiring someone who will be respected and honored by your Board.

Choosing Your Event

There are three main categories of special events: we'll call them the House Social, the Theme/Extravaganza, and the Public Party. The **House Social** is a party for people who already know you, already love you, and probably know a little (or a lot!) about each other. They will also pay medium-to-big ticket prices. This event generally takes the form of an awards dinner, a bring-the-kids special holiday party, a black-tie dinner with entertainment, and so on. This is when your "family" comes together to have some fun, spend some money, congratulate each other, and, often, wear beautiful or outrageous clothes.

The **Theme/Extravaganza** is an event so good, so hot, that it doesn't matter who you are. This category includes things like house/garden/studio tours, film premieres, and a host of theme-related expositions, performances, demonstrations and "celebrity opportunities".

The **Public Party** is an activity that people will do (or something they will buy) anyway, and your presence will help influence

This is no time to offer an internship.

...an event so hot it doesn't matter who you are

191

when or where they do it. Examples include special or "percentage" days at theme parks, street fairs, family sports days, and an appalling array of a-thons.

RULE OF THUMB: Your event may be doomed to fail if, at the very first planning meeting, you cannot name a certain percentage of your guest list before you even start. For the House Social, you must be able to **name** 50% of your guests; for a Theme/Extravaganza, 35% will do. For a Public Party, you should be able to name 25% of your participant-guests, have a good community base and some indication of broad-based interest and support.

...the 50% - 35% - 25% rule

How can you possibly do this? You can do this by answering these three questions:

❖ What are the results of your feasibility study?

❖ Do you really have agreement to do the event?
  This means: This is a Board (not a staff) event, and the Board is 100% committed to doing it. Specifically, each Board member has agreed to take a major chunk of work (and to be available for x hours/week for x weeks) **and** has committed to sell tickets, bring their friends, spend money appropriately, and whatever else your event requires.

❖ Can you pull it off exquisitely?
  This means: Do you have enough enthusiastic core volunteers? Is there some enthusiasm in the community, particularly from potential donors and underwriters? Do you have a good prospective guest/participant list or know where to get it? Do you have the money to meet pre-event expenses?

You need 100% Board commitment.

192

More about Feasibility

Using the model described in detail in "How To Do A Feasibility Study," you should fease your event. As you will recall from our example of the Houseboat Tours, feasing a brand-new event is absolutely essential; you will also find it useful to check up on your annual event by feasing new ideas or twists — if you have not been evaluating your event over the years, this will be a gold mine of information.

Basically, you want to find out if you are on track with your event idea by surveying people both inside and outside your family. You want to know: Do people like the idea and want to pay to come? Do potential vital donors, underwriters and sponsors express real interest? Can your community handle it — police, parking, etc.? For this part you will fease potential donors and underwriters, potential attendees, media folks, relevant civic groups and leaders — the Police Chief, the Mayor, the head of Parks and Recreation. For your internal fease you will ask the musical question: Is this a party **you** are panting to attend? If the answer is no, then you are definitely giving the wrong party. A good idea for your internal survey is to ask core volunteers and staff to each write, secretly, what they would most like at the party, and what would it take to get them to go if they were not affiliated with your organization.

As always, follow the format faithfully. As always, you must be objective about your idea: do not defend it but rather listen to your feasees — you have chosen them because they'll tell you

Is this a party you are panting to attend? If not, you are throwing the wrong party.

193

the truth. As always, the feasing process will bring you potential volunteers, potential guests/participants, an involvement or stake in the event by folks who could have been trouble, and reams of good ideas on the details.

Setting Goals

When you have answered the first three questions satisfactorily, then you can begin setting goals for your event. What is its purpose — new friends, new money, more money from current donors, community acceptance, consciousness-raising? What do you want the event to accomplish for your organization? How much money will you plan to make? How many people do you plan to reach? Each major piece of the event — Underwriting & Sponsorships, Ticket Sales, Public Relations & Advertising, Food & Drink, Item Solicitation . . . whatever you need — will have internal goals, too.

Each piece of the event will have specific goals.

DO NOT DO THIS, OR ANY OTHER EVENT UNLESS:
❖ You have a great, great idea (remember, you are **entertainment**, competing in a tough entertainment world)
❖ It is new or has an important twist (but, no jumping on someone else's great idea!)
❖ You have clear goals
❖ Everybody you know already wants to come (the 50% - 35% - 25% rule)
❖ You have enough time (12 weeks minimum, more for most events)

* You have enough volunteers to do it right (your core group, not day-of-event folks)
* You plan to do it more than once (the First Annual is always hardest)
* You are willing to pay attention to 400 details

The Event Budget

Make it realistic, even generous. Include the cost of everything, even if you are working on underwriting. You may have to pay for it this time or next. Include all the details you can foresee: insurance, extra hires, invitations, hall rental — the little expenses as well as the big ones. Also include staff costs. Nobody will like this, because it usually plunges your net below acceptable limits, but do it anyway. Remember, and remind your Board: time spent on this event is not spent on program. Set revenue goals in each category that will stretch but not dismay your volunteers. Never say, "Get as many sponsorships as you can," or "Sell as many tickets as you can." Setting goals helps to put the event in perspective and makes the divisions of responsibility possible.

Then, make sure that everybody agrees on the general budget line, knowing that there will be changes in categories and items as solicitation goes on. Second, give over the purse strings of each category to the Chair or Task Force leader responsible. Make it easy for them to access their budgeted funds. Task

**Confession:
The Worst Event I've Ever Done I**

One year, while I was still behind a desk, my Board of Directors decided to try something new – something besides the 2005th annual auction/dinner which was still successful but not growing as it should. They decided to sponsor a stock car race at a local and rather famous raceway. The idea was, we could get a percentage of all the tickets we sold and would add little extras like meeting race car drivers and such. Entirely in

195

Force and Team leaders, and all their volunteers, should know what the budget is, what flexibility there is, and where the lines of communication are connected.

Choosing The Team

There must be one person in charge of your event who **knows, not does** everything. This person must be powerful within your family (this is not a learning experience), able and willing to wear out a telephone, not going to Fiji within the next six months, on excellent terms with your staff, persistent and vicious. This person can be a Board member or a community volunteer. To be named Chairperson of your event is an honor, a prize. If you have to beg, you're asking the wrong person.

Once you have the leader, **then** choose the rest of your team. There should be one major staff liaison — the Director of Development if you have one. If you do not, make this staff assignment carefully: be sure this person is released from some of his or her usual work, and that the entire staff understands and supports this. Also, get the whole secretarial thing straightened out right now: who will do event work and how will you plug the hole? Look at each category of work, and write a job description for the Task Force (or whatever) leaders before you recruit them.

Now you are ready to recruit the rest of your team. Look at each category of work, count how many volunteers you think

addition to the highly unsatisfactory deal they made with the raceway owner was our total inability to sell tickets to this turkey! Who goes to the car races? Lots of wonderful folks, but we didn't know any of them. (see Choosing Your Event) Even worse than that was the race day itself. There we were, a pitiful few, huddled under a canopy...the band playing, a few brave champagne corks popping, when a VERY famous actor-driver (get it?) spun out RIGHT IN FRONT OF US and damn near died RIGHT THERE in front of the Mental Health tent. He, being a great driver, controlled his car and lived. We went back to the Auction.

you will need, then double that number. Write job descriptions for each job. Include emphases on deadlines, how and with whom to communicate, expectations, limitations and rules. (Although whoever does "it" gets to say what "it" looks like, you can avoid disaster by laying down a few guidelines: I'll never forget the time a volunteer went off to design the invitation and get it done for free, only to bring it back, all printed and ready to go, in the colors of a not-quite-rival organization!)

Make a profile of the perfect volunteer for the job, then look at who you have and recruit them directly, job description in hand. This includes Board members, friends, staff, program volunteers. Then, widen your circle to volunteers' friends and family, your membership and clients, civic groups with appropriate focus, and strangers off the street (see Working With Volunteers).

This is not, in general, a time for teaching. There are exceptions, of course: Task Force leaders can teach new volunteers if they meet other requirements. NO CLASS PROJECTS! Another experience I'll never forget was the time a volunteer delivered 250 bid-number cards for a fancy auction. They had been made with love by her class — unfortunately, it was the third grade.

Volunteer Recruitment, Training and Appreciation

Whether you are recruiting by word of mouth, stories in your newsletter, or advertisements in the paper the requirements are

---

Eleven Event Rules Never To Be Broken No Matter What
(read, then add your own)

1. Remember that this is a party, not a life sentence.
2. The event is headed by one person, paid or unpaid, who knows EVERYTHING.
3. No unnecessary meetings!
4. No free tickets!!!
5. Feed the press!
6. NEVER give away the bar.
7. Have a BUDGET and GOALS.
8. Evaluate in writing.
9. Get the name and address of EVERYBODY there.
10. NEVER plan an event that depends for its whole success on the performance of children, animals or the weather.
11. Whoever does "it" gets to say what "it" looks like.

the same: your volunteers must already know how to give a great party; must be able to pay attention to detail; must want, really want, to do the job; must be able to do it; and must have an answering machine.

As you screen volunteers, be prepared to assign them to appropriate jobs, sometimes with great tact.

When you have a reasonable number of volunteers, start your team-building. Have a meeting — make it more like a party — outside the office if possible, where team leaders and all of your core volunteers meet each other, learn and tell what they will do, and learn the basics of the event. Then **they** design the party. (Don't worry about day-of-event volunteers just yet — you'll recruit and train them later.) If your prospective volunteers don't seem to want to come to the meeting, they probably don't really want to volunteer. Make this first party, and one two or check-up meetings along the way, part of the job.

Make attractive volunteer packets and update them throughout the season. Make sure everyone knows the overall event structure and time-line, knows where to get the things they need, and knows who's supposed to be doing what and with whom.

For some ideas on honoring volunteers, read "Working With Volunteers." Event preparation often covers several months, so you also need to find ways to cheer folks up along the way.

They design the party.

Make the kick-off and check-up meetings part of the job.

Confession:
The Worst Event I've Ever Done II

It was my first. It was a Community Fair, in our parking lot – the parking lot of the free clinic. We had home-made game booths and local musicians and an Old West theme. We had gotten soap and fruit juice coupons and other highly valuable items to be raffled off. I had talked the rest of the Clinic staff into wearing Old West clothes I got donated. So there we were, all in costume: mine was a hot-pink satin dress trimmed with black lace and draped with a black feather boa.

A word about "Honorary" Chairpersons, Committees, etc.: Sometimes this is a very good idea. It's a great way of reaching out to parts of the community you don't ordinarily reach. But, you must:

❖ Be very clear about what you want your Honorary folks to do. Do you want them to donate money? Must they show up? Are they requested to invite other people? How many? How many (if any) complimentary tickets will you offer?

❖ Watch carefully for an overload of Honorary folks — if you have too many nobody will believe they're all devotees of your organization, and if you have (against our best advice) decided to offer free tickets you may insult your paying guests.

❖ Be sure to honor your real Chairpeople loud and clear.

Underwriting and Sponsorship

Whatever your event, you can and should have a cash sponsorship program. This means that corporations, businesses, interest groups, and individuals give you money in return for mention in your program or other vehicle. Sometimes sponsorships include a set number of tickets: if the ticket price is $25, a $250 sponsorship includes two tickets, the $500 level gets four, etc. But do not give away the store. THIS IS YOUR ABSOLUTE BEST WAY TO MAKE MONEY ON ANY EVENT. Think about it.

> *I looked like Miss Kitty's aging hippie niece. Now, I've had fourteen years to think about this event, and I **know** that we would have broken even except for the fact that the event ended in a fistfight and we got blood on our costumes and had to have them dry-cleaned. Otherwise we would have made close to one hundred dollars. I learned many lessons from this, the most important one being, and I bring this to you in all sincerity: Never give away the beer.*

Underwriting is just a fancy way of describing a cash gift that is earmarked to fund one piece of your event. Most often a corporation or business will agree to pay for one piece (printing, transportation, sound equipment — don't snigger, I lost a fancy microphone once and it cost $350 to replace it!) of your event in exchange for appropriate mention in the program, your publicity pieces and the like. Occasionally a corporation will underwrite the expenses of an entire event. Before you approach corporations with this idea, have some idea yourself of what the corporation might consider fair return for a large chunk of change. Make an attractive shopping list, just as you do for other corporate solicitation.

The sponsorship/underwriting Task Force is probably the most important of the lot; it needs an extremely persistent leader, and volunteers who are already not afraid to ask. Set clear, achievable goals with this Task Force. Most times, individual sponsorships come in different categories than corporate ones; in your personal sponsorship drive, set reasonable categories so that all your Board members can sponsor on some level.

Set reasonable categories so that each Board member can sponsor your event.

If possible, name early sponsors and underwriters in the invitation. By all means, spend the money (if you have to) on a post-event display ad in the paper your business sponsors read.

Ticket Sales

RULE # ONE: Advertising does not sell tickets. Even a great

Only people sell tickets.

200

idea does not sell tickets. Only people sell tickets.

I can hear you right now: "But I've designed such a great event it will sell itself!" Not true. You are not Ticketron. Even if you have the absolute hottest event in the world, you must have a superb distribution/media/outreach plan. And by and large, you will need to encourage people to come to your party by inviting them in a very personal way.

In addition to selling tickets one by one (the hard way), you could do one or both of the following:

❖ Encourage every single Board member, volunteer and staff person to put together a group of friends who will come to the event and sit at "their" table or participate together in some way. You can also sell tables or ticket blocks to civic groups, corporations and businesses.

❖ Encourage every single Board member, volunteer and staff person to give a personal, pre-event "outreach" party where friends learn about the event early on and buy in. I thought I invented this, of course. One year while I was producing an auction, I feared we would be short of items — our champion item-getter was on sabbatical in Switzerland. So I invited a group of friends to brunch, pitched them about the auction (those who had been to one praised it to the newcomers), and asked them to make a special effort to donate items from their own collections (jewelry and prints, mostly). Well, it worked. Every woman at the lunch became my partner in the auction. That group produced some of the finest (and funniest) items

You are not Ticketron.

we ever had. Not only that, but every single one bought at least two tickets, came to the party, spent money and had a wonderful time, and left thinking about what they might donate the next year. I felt great because they had had fun. They felt great because they "owned" a piece of the event.

It is perfectly okay, in fact it is imperative, that everyone in your organization be expected to sell tickets — unless it is such a pricey event that only a few lucky souls can afford it. If your Board is dragging its collective feet on ticket sales to the event, better find out why. There is probably something else going on here.

SECRET: You already know this one. The only 100% foolproof way to sell tickets to a House Social, or even a Theme/Extravaganza, is to have Board and volunteers buy a bunch of tickets. You hold their check, returning it when they bring their ticket money in.

Timelines and Managing the Details

If you are the person in charge of tracking all this, set up an "Event Central" as soon as decently possible. Make it pretty, even if it's just a corner in the Board room. Set up your supplies, telephones, electronics well in advance of the first flurry of activity. When the group has agreed on the timeline, the Task Forces and their composition, and the goals for the overall event and each revenue-producing section, make charts

...set up "Event Central" as soon as decently possible

and hang them right there on the wall. Make it easy for volunteers to come by and pick up information and supplies, deliver donations, and find out what's going on.

Set up all your systems: tracking of every single soul and donation; plans for donor recognition; plans for volunteer cheerleading and appreciation; and, more important than you can possibly imagine, make **two copies of everything and put them somewhere safe.**

Why might I say this? Well, I didn't always.

Confession: Remember the Houseboat Tour? Well, we were just steaming along, figuring out how to manage an event that would take 200 volunteers to pull it off, reveling in the organization's new computer. Not a care in the world. Well, ten days before the event, the damn building burned down. To the ground. And with everything else, along went our three-color bus/pier/houseboat logistics plans, diagrams and all, along with the names and telephone numbers of all the volunteers and the donations we had already received and the directions for picking up the food donated from twenty restaurants . . . you get the picture. Actually, everybody was wonderful and the event was a huge success. People picked their way through the ashes carrying cases of wine, saying, "I read about you in the paper and thought this might help." But it was a hard way to learn a very simple lesson.

Although you'll mail invitations four to five weeks before a social event, put an invitation to the event on your office and home answering machines early on. Get other volunteers and staff to do it, too.

Start making the Event Book right away, and add to it constantly. It will be the official reflection of the event, and will contain samples of everything, all the lists, letters, contracts, and so forth. Do it faithfully: you could get hit by a bus.

Keep to the rule of NO UNNECESSARY MEETINGS. Encourage people to get together not just to share information, but only to make decisions. Task Force leaders are in charge of their volunteers. You can schedule a mid-way check-in party or two for all the volunteers to share progress and encourage each other.

Donor Treatment

If a letter is requested or needed, write a really good one and add the personal touch. Don't drown your potential donors/sponsors/underwriters in paper. Describe your event briefly but cheerfully, make a specific request, name the time when you will follow it up; then do it, calling the prospect and writing everything down.

Feature your major donors as fully and graciously as you can at your event, through displays, splashy recognition in the

Do the Event Book faithfully: you could get hit by a bus.

No speeches, please.

204

program, whatever it takes. But no speeches, please. An introduction and brief thank you, if necessary.

When you thank your donors, thank them as specifically as you solicited them. Use some humor, some kind of light touch; again, don't drown them in paper. Report briefly on the success of your event and their part in it. Include copies of news articles and your thank-you ad.

...thank donors specifically

One last word about donor relations: Ask your entire organizational family — Board, staff, volunteers, clients, party guests — to support businesses which have supported you and, further, to take the extra time and trouble to tell the owner or manager why they are doing so. Of course this goes for any kind of business/non-profit relationship, but local businesses, especially, often feel taken for granted when they support special events.

...support businesses which have supported you

Analysis and Evaluation

This is an essential part of your event. In the analysis, you want to find out not only how much money you made, but also how you made it and why. You want to find out what event elements did or did not work, if they can be fixed, and how to fix them. I suggest you go about this in three ways, as soon as possible after the event. Get everything done within three weeks or you will lose valuable input.

1) First, do the numbers and take stock. Because your record-keeping has of course been impeccable, you should have all the information at hand. Crunch all the numbers, big and little, and do not fudge. Be fair and honest. Watch out for both the rosy glow that follows a great party and the awful gloom that follows an ill-fated event. In your analysis, trace the source of each dollar made (and spent). This way you can find out what parts of your design and which members of your team were really on the money.

Crunch all the numbers, and don't fudge.

2) Conduct a small post-event telephone survey of selected guests, major donors, major in-kind contributors, and non-core volunteers. This is a little tricky. First, figure out exactly what you want to know (just like the feasibility study), then choose people who you think will tell you the truth. Decide whether you can make the call or if you will need some help. Through this survey, you'll want to find out things like: Did major contributors feel appreciated before and during the event? What did your guests really like or dislike about the party? Were the arrangements for participants (particularly in a-thons or other active events) adequate and friendly? Would the respondent attend/volunteer again next year? Keep your questions (and the whole conversation) brief but to the point; start your conversation with appreciation for your respondent's participation in the event, a spirited comment about how you're already looking at next year, and a pledge of confidentiality. In the case of major underwriters, in-kind donors, etc., you may want to make this survey an integral part of your thank-you process. Were the publicity arrangements satisfactory? Did the

Figure out exacly what you want to know.

...find out how your community partnership is really working

borrowed costumes get delivered in one piece by courteous volunteers? You get the point: this is not necessarily the time to get your donors' commitment to next year, but it is the time to let your community know you care about the quality of response and attention your organization is giving out — how the community partnership is really working.

3) Have a celebration meeting as soon as possible with the core volunteers and/or whoever in the organization really worked on and cared about the event. You will of course share your crunched numbers and the results of your tiny survey with this group. Congratulate each other, by all means give silly prizes and recognize accomplishments, then agree on total confidentiality and critique the event by asking the following questions:

❖ Who supported this event?

❖ Who bought tickets, and who actually came?

❖ Did you meet your attendance/income goals?

❖ To what extent was the Board involved? Staff? Volunteers?

❖ How well was your event organized? Did the structure work? Who actually did the work of each committee/task force?

❖ How much did the event cost? How much did the event cost if staff time is factored into the equation?

❖ What went right with each part/element/section? What went wrong?

❖ Does this event fit your organization?

❖ WAS IT WORTH IT?

Celebrate!

Confession:
I remember the year that Lily Tomlin agreed to MC the program for a black-tie dinner. Jimmy Carter was running for president. Our most well-connected board member arranged for "Miss Lillian" Carter to make an appearance. Miss Lillian showed up about halfway through the dinner. She walked through the hall and a ripple of giggles started along with the applause. No one knew what was happening until she got to the stage. When she stood up to honor the person we were honoring, she had on the exact

After all this is done, and your numbers are solid, take your and the group's recommendations on the event to the whole Board. Make a summary sheet, and have the worksheets available for those who are interested. Now, do not file this evaluation too far back in the drawer. Put it in your Event Book. You'll need it — for reality checks, for ideas for next year, for ammunition.

same dress as Lily Tomlin. Lily, thank God, was laughing but Miss Lillian still didn't know what was funny.

How to Do An Auction

There are three basic kinds of auctions:

1) The "Bargain Hunter's Dream" where you offer an array of services, collectibles, probably some art, and a few major items such as trips;

2) The "$2,000 Duck Dinner" where your wealthier donors enjoy highly competitive bidding on creative treats, slightly-used luxury cars, and expensive wine and art;

3) The "Specialty Auction" where only one or two kinds of items are offered.

All three can make money, but you must be entirely realistic about your audience. All auctions are really House Socials (see How to Choose Your Event); even if you choose a "Specialty Auction", you must be able to **name** more than half of your guests at your first Task Force meeting! The "Bargain Hunter's Dream" can appeal to a fairly large range of donors -- you can feature items that will sell in every price range -- and is the most volunteer-intensive of the three. Try the "$2,000 Duck Dinner" **only** if your donors are wealthy AND like to be seen spending money in public.

You may not do this unless:

❖ You are in a community where people like to come to events, **and** there are not too many auctions already fixed in community folklore.

❖ You can get **great, imaginative** big-ticket items.

❖ You have a **beloved, talented** local celebrity auctioneer--or even a team of them. Professional auctioneers, although they help speed up the process and know the value of the items they're selling, are in our experience absolutely no match for the ones who will relate personally to bidders.

❖ Your "Specialty" items are so unusual or so rare or so exciting that you can appeal to an audience far beyond your regular one. For example, a local high school theater group auctions off "Celebrity Doodles", framed and signed. We're talking big names here. The annual Wine Auction, sponsored by growers, vintners and others in the Napa Valley, attracts people literally from around the world, and makes a ton of money for a group of non-profits in the area. Choose a specialty auction only if you have a **great** source for items, like a real collector who wants to donate his entire hoard of Star Trek memorabilia, **and** you can publicize your event handsomely.

Many auctions have two parts: the "Silent" and the "Grand". A Silent Auction features items displayed on tables or easels, with paper bid slips attached. Guest circulate among the items, writing their bid numbers an the amount they are bidding on the slips. The "Grand" is the live auction: items are displayed and sold one by one.

Always build your auction around food-and-drink. You can have a sit-down dinner, with a silent Auction going on during the cocktail hour and the Grand Auction beginning during the dessert course. This is probably the best approach if you have an extensive live auction and lots of big ticket items. You always get more money for any item if your bidders are sitting down!

You will need:
❖ a wonderful, inviting place with plenty of room for item display
❖ good food (and lots of it) and decent wine
❖ a large number of persistent volunteers who will get good items
❖ a host of well-trained event volunteers: cashiers, table monitors, runners, bid-spotters, item packers, etc.
❖ at least six months lead time
❖ item storage

If you are giving a "Bargain Hunter's Dream" you will need lots of people and lots of items to make any money on the auction floor. Like most events, your real money will be made on personal, business and corporate sponsorships. It helps to have guidelines about the types and quality of items you will accept: this helps your business donors to think you're really organized **and** it gets your volunteers off the hook when they are offered cheap or tacky gifts. You are looking for a good balance between collectibles, art, specialty items, and services. By all means include traditional and imaginative services in your auction: folks love to bid on things they'll buy anyway -- dinners for two or four, automotive tune-ups, flower delivery and so on. If you know your audience, you'll be able to please them even more: if they are pet fanciers, go for certificates for dog grooming, portraits of pets and owners, stays at pet "hotels" to accompany the wonderful get-away weekends you're offering.

A serious word of advice: be very careful of how you offer personal services. For some reason, they tend not to sell very well, so: 1) you won't make very much money, and 2) if the donor is in the audience he or she might be embarrassed. Avoid, for example: fundraising consultation, psychotherapy, wardrobe/closet/decorating consultation, dental work, accordion lessons, funeral planning, and legal work of any kind!

Do offer whimsical, "priceless" gifts from the most well-known and respected people in your "family". Our favorite one is "Grandparents For a Night" where the most beloved child care experts in our community offer a mini-vacation with great treats for two or three children. Actually, grown-ups have been known to bid on this, too -- holding the "grandparents" to their promise of roasted marshmallows and stories by the fire.

Exquisite donor treatment is essential to any auction. In addition to really good request letters (in which you will ask for a specific donation or offer one or two choices), you'll want to write highly personalized thank-yous to your individual and business donors. For big items, tell them who bought it, if you can; say how much you enjoyed having it around the office (or house) before the event; try to give some flavor of the party. And, of course, encourage all your volunteers and guests to patronize businesses which support you **and** to again express their appreciation when they redeem certificates, etc.

CHAPTER THIRTEEN
How to Work (With) the Media

Scandal as News

At a recent meeting of non-profit managers and media executives the question of attracting coverage was addressed. Why aren't non-profits newsworthy? If our major newspapers and television stations cover dog and boat shows, beauty pageants, and endless stories about blood and gore, why is there no place for the good human work we are doing?

...boat shows, beauty pageants, blood and gore abound

The media executives told the non-profit managers that the only time non-profits are newsworthy is when they are embroiled in scandal.

So the bookkeeper runs away with the petty cash, the payroll taxes have not been paid and the feds are dragging out the furniture, and the secretary of the Board is sleeping with the mayor. That means front page news. And how does the community react? They read every word and then say, "Ah ha, I knew they were a bunch of bums." In the meantime, these "bums" are helping teenagers kick their drug habits and bringing classical music to kindergardeners in the ghetto. But that rarely reaches the public.

...But when the bookkeeper runs away with the petty cash: "I knew they were a bunch of bums!"

The inability to tell our stories through the media is very frustrating. It means that when we go out to ask for money some people we are approaching have never heard of us. It means that the good people who work and volunteer in non-profit organizations are devalued by the media that supposedly show society what is "important" to see. That clearly is not you. The only way right now for many non-profits to get space in the newspapers and on radio and television is to buy time, and then answer to funding sources for high overhead costs.

It is distressing to face this fact, but face it we must. If we are to change media priorities and place the non-profit sector on the national agenda, you must make the time to educate the media. With all else you have to do, this project seems to be a low priority. But as long as non-profits shake fists at the media from afar you will be left off television screens and out of the newspapers, and therefore remain second class citizens in the communities you serve.

...face it we must

A Different Approach

"EDUCATING THE MEDIA" does not mean:
- sending them mountains of materials they never read
- badgering or preaching to them
- shot-gunning long-winded press releases to every newspaper on your list
- ignoring their deadlines
- having media coverage as an after thought

"Educate" means cultivate, involve and inform.

SOME IDEAS on how to do that are:

❖ Put a television executive on your Board.

❖ Ask the local newspaper publisher to serve as chair of the PR committee for one year.

❖ Write your own feature stories complete with great black and white photographs and "sell" them to the local weeklies looking for stories as fillers.

❖ Instead of inviting the press to your Open House or Auction or Opening as an afterthought, create a special press event complete with food, beverages and well-structured press kits.

❖ Read the papers and watch TV to find out which reporters do a lot of "human interest" stories and what their pet causes are. They are the ones you want to approach.

❖ If your organization needs something, let your local media know about it. In Tampa, Florida, a Head Start program had all of their toys ripped off in a burglary. A call to a TV reporter resulted in a delivery of left-over but new toys from "Toys for Tots". Great coverage for both organizations!

❖ Let reporters know about outstanding volunteers - they make great human interest stories. Did one of your volunteers go out of his way to invent a "gizmo" that makes life easier for the disabled person he visits? Has someone spent 15 years building the sets for all of your plays? Is there a special success story that one of your clients is willing to tell?

❖ Invite reporters, especially columnists, to do an

"involvement" story: invite them to help cook and serve the Thanksgiving meal at your soup kitchen; let them ride along on a "Meals on Wheels" delivery run; give them a chance to help "coach" the Special Olympics.

❖ Send regular press releases and PSA's, in the proper format, to announce all of the great things you are doing: "Russian Ballerinas Attend Special Showing of Ancient Icons"; "Clinic Chosen to Test New Vaccine"; "1000th Puppy Placed with Hearing-Impaired Child."   You may hit a nerve and attract some more major coverage. Remember, because you are not (I hope) literally on fire, you cannot expect reporters to come to you looking for news.

❖ Non-profits and the media need each other. If you get the opportunity to be friends with a local reporter, go for it! And for heaven's sake, share your access with your colleagues in other non-profits!

If you think of the media as another client base, as another audience, and as part of your community, and structure your program to meet their needs, all non-profits and the people they serve will benefit from the positive exposure you generate.

How to Produce an Awards Banquet

An Awards Banquet is not a roast (taking painful jabs at someone everyone loves), a black tie dinner, an auction or any other primary fundraising activity. However, it may take any form: barbecue, rubber chicken dinner, finger sandwich luncheon, spectacular dessert party, great hors d'oeuvres, cocktail party, etc. The key ingredient here is honor: community leaders, volunteer of the year, a renowned artist/ author/ doctor within your field.

You throw an Awards Banquet to actually honor someone(s), to bring new people into your non-profit family (usually the family and friends of the honoree), and to have fun and get good press. Depending on who you honor, you might raise money. You may not charge too much for the tickets, leaving the community and the family and friends of the honoree unable to attend. However, a good rule of thumb is that, unless you are rolling in dough, the event must at least break even. Remember, you can use the sale of ads in the program and corporate underwriting to make money, too.

This is one of the few events where you may want to offer special ticket prices. Still, Event Rule #1 still applies: only the honoree(s) and the press get in for free.

What you need

The most important element is to be very careful about who you honor. Do not honor anyone who is very controversial unless you are ready for the negative feedback (and remember you could lose donors who are insulted by your choice). Stay away from honoring politicians unless they are dead because everyone will either love or hate them. Really know why this person deserves an award. Remember the five stages of a project:

1) Enthusiasm
2) Disillusionment
3) Panic
4) Search for the guilty
5) Punishment of the innocent
6) Praise and honors for non-participants

Make sure that you are not doing #6.

Details to Consider:

❖ The award itself may not be a plaque or trophy from the same mold as the Little League's. It must be something unique that the honoree will be proud to display. The award may either be institutional, which means, like the Oscars, the trophy is the same year after year, or it could be specific to the person, like a bronzed cover of their latest book.

❖ If one of your goals is to make the press, make sure that the honoree is newsworthy. This can be discovered beforehand through your feasibility study.

❖ Pay great attention to the guest list. Make sure that key people from your field are invited, and make sure to invite the honoree's guest list.

❖ Create a nice party at a convenient time and place. Saturday night is asking too much of your guests. Lunch during the week is generally better. It depends on your community.

Twists

You could take a "Golden Fleece" approach and "honor" the worst and most contemptible: corporations that rape the environment, authors who miss the point on battering women, art critics. Just don't expect them to show up. But be ready in case they do.

❖ It might work in your community to have community-wide balloting for the Volunteer of the Year.

❖ You might try a "This is Your Life" Award, especially if the honoree is very beloved and an integral part of the fabric of your community.

❖ It always helps an event if you hold it in a place that people want to see. Then some people will then come because it's you giving the event, some will come because of the honoree, and some will come to see the place: a magnificent home, a not-yet-opened swanky hotel or department store, a private rose garden, etc.

CHAPTER FOURTEEN
Working with Volunteers

Actually, volunteers in fundraising are big business. More than one in every four people over the age of 13 volunteer, and Gallup reports that even more (70%) are willing to volunteer. Traditional youth groups and Big Diseases have literally millions of volunteers each. Using volunteers in program, planning and fundraising keeps us cost-effective and alive. So why do so many non-profits complain about the lack of volunteers or the ineffectiveness of the ones they've got?

In many cases, working with volunteers becomes difficult because tasks are vague, lines of authority and communication are muddled and volunteers are either under-appreciated or gushed over inappropriately. A general rule of thumb is that one-third of your volunteers are **leaders** and will take the initiative to get things done; one-third are good **followers** and will carry on very well, given good leadership; and one-third are **flakes** and will never follow through no matter what. So, volunteers must be honored, not only for their accomplishments, but also by having your act together in terms of planning, materials and leadership.

Here are some guidelines to help you attract, keep and honor the kinds of volunteers you need.

...volunteers are either underappreciated or gushed over inappropriately

*Volunteers must be honored not only for their accomplishments but also by having **your** act together.*

219

Step One: Find Them

First, decide what you want your volunteers to do. Plan and produce a dinner? Follow up a direct mail piece with a phonathon? Hustle items for your crafts auction? Make a list, then write a two-sentence description for each volunteer job. Then you are ready to begin recruiting volunteers, and you will be less inclined to soft-pedal the requirements or the scope of the jobs.

Of course, you'll recruit first by word of mouth — among your Board, staff and current volunteers. You'll ask friends and colleagues, too, to look at your list and see if there's a place there for them.

Then you'll broaden your approach. By all means, register with your local Volunteer Bureau, but keep in mind that it's okay to screen and refuse anyone they send you if you think it won't work. Then go a step further: Advertise! Run an ad in the classified section: "If you know how to give a great party, a volunteer job in our agency is waiting for you! We need special decorations, public relations and advertising know-how and energy, and people to help solicit great auction items. Call us for details." The people who read want ads are either out of work and trying to figure out how to break into a field, or dissatisfied with their present job and seeing what else is out there. In either case, you are offering the volunteer a great opportunity to add a successful piece of work to their resume.

What do you want them to do?

"If you know how to throw a great party..."

You can also advertise in specialized publications that feature staff and volunteer positions in your area. In these publications, advertise your volunteer opportunity with the same care and precision you'd use for a paid-staff position. When folks call to answer any of your ads, find out where they read about you and what prompted them to respond. Which job is he or she applying for? Then make a timely appointment for a get-acquainted interview where you and the prospective volunteer will see if there's a "match".

...advertise with care and precision

Step Two: Use Them Well

The two most important things you must offer a volunteer up front, in addition to graciousness and a sincere interest in him or her, are a full job description and appropriate training. And, as you interview your prospective volunteers, you must share your expectations honestly — not downplaying either the responsibilities or the difficulty of the job. You must be as willing to say "no" to a prospective volunteer as you are to a candidate interviewing for a paid job. (It is also okay to put them on a waiting list if you have no need for their skills at that moment.)

...you must be willing to say no

Volunteer job descriptions should be written with a fairly light touch, but should nonetheless be written. Make sure you include:

❖ exactly what the task is

❖ exactly when it must be done: Deadlines!

❖ suggestions and rules for how to do it

❖ budget and how it is accessed

❖ lines of authority: committee chair, staff liaison. etc.

Volunteer training can take a variety of forms. I recommend training volunteers in groups whenever possible, so they can get that wonderful team feeling as well as an exchange of ideas, followed up when necessary with one-to-one sessions. Remember here an important rule: **whoever does "it" gets to say what "it" looks like**. So don't back your volunteers into a corner by "training" them only to do it the same way you've done it for centuries — you invited them in to give you new energy and ideas, right? Familiarize them with the work and standards of your organization, give them parameters within which to work, offer them a contract that makes sense, welcome them warmly to your family, then let them go and do their jobs.

Most volunteer fundraising jobs should come with a Volunteer Packet, an attractive, informative and personalized "bunch of stuff" they will need. Make sure you include:

A complete description of the event/activity/campaign
If applicable, last year's invitation/press clippings/program
A complete time-line
A personalized letter of introduction to prospective donors
Committee lists, Board list and agency brochure
Job description
A hearty thank-you

...don't "train" them only to do it the same way you've done it for centuries

Each time you launch a volunteer-intensive effort, check yourself on these important details:

❖ Have you chosen volunteers who already know how to throw a great party/speak in front of groups/write great letters?

❖ Does everybody have a job description? Do they know how their jobs fit in the big picture? Have they agreed to do that job?

❖ Has every volunteer been trained?

❖ Is there a clear beginning, middle and end?

❖ Do you have all the information you need **from** the volunteer?

❖ Do you have all the information you need **for** the volunteer?

❖ Are there scheduled check-ups along the way?

❖ Are there clear lines of authority?

❖ Have you planned how to honor your volunteers?

Following the "job" model for volunteers, please note that you may indeed have to fire one of them! In fact, you must fire them if they are not doing their job: this whole thing is about raising money to allow your valuable work to go forward; it is not about abandoning professionalism because someone's feelings might get hurt. What I find works best, when a volunteer is faltering or is missing deadlines to the detriment of the campaign, is first to find out what's wrong. Maybe there's a piece of information that will fix the problem. If that doesn't work, then I set some mini-deadlines for the volunteer to meet, and call him or her often to see how it's going. If it's still not working out, then I thank them for their effort and gently but

...find out what's wrong

223

clearly take the task away and give it to someone else. I find that the volunteer, rather than being angry, is usually relieved.

Using the "job" model, however, you will more often than not have successful volunteers: they'll know what they're signing on to do, will feel respected by your professional approach to their talents, and it will be a complete win-win situation.

Step Three: Thank Them

I expect that, by now, I don't have to repeat how important this is. But since one-third of our volunteers tend to be leaders, another third followers, and the final third dead wood, where organizations get into trouble is in dealing with all of these people the same way.

The famous Six Steps of a Project should be reviewed here:
1) Enthusiasm
2) Disillusionment
3) Panic
4) Search for the guilty
5) Punishment of the innocent
6) Praise and honors for non-participants

This progression is entirely too true when it comes to thanking volunteers. I believe that the problem is that we tend to be so bloody grateful that anyone even bothered to show up to help that we get confused about how to reward the three different

...we tend to be so bloody grateful that we get confused

224

types of volunteers and we get caught in #6 above. Here are some suggestions for approaching your three different types of participants:

DEAD WOOD. Thank them with a letter for offering to help. Do not credit them with any activity for which they volunteered but did not work. Then take out your clipboard labeled "People Never To Be Trusted With Responsibility Again" and add their name to it. In other words, GET RID OF THEM!

This "dead wood" category gets complicated when the dead wood in question is either a donor, somebody's mother/spouse/consort, a Board member, or some supposedly powerful person in your community. I recently did a training for a very large arts organization that absolutely balked, sputtered and fumed when I suggested that they remove anyone from the Auxiliary who is not showing up to help with their event. "Are you kidding?" they shouted almost in unison. "Our biggest donor is proud to be listed in that group, even though he hasn't shown up since 1962. You want us to say **what** to him?"

Okay, so it's not so very cut-and-dried. But the best model for a functioning group that I've found is the 100% active model. People like to belong to a group where everyone pulls his or her own weight, the volunteer activity is so exciting that it can be seen moving in the right direction, and everyone feels utterly appreciated. This cannot happen if you set up a system in which some folks work and others are let off the hook for whatever reason. You would be compromising the integrity of

"Are you kidding?"

...the best model is the 100% active model

the group, and once that happens you'll see the fabric of commitment and energy start to unravel.

Think about all of your volunteer jobs, including the Board. What is your price for a Board seat? Does a $10,000 donor get a seat and excused from meetings? How about $9000? What is your price for undermining your volunteer effort?

FOLLOWERS. As soon as you identify a volunteer as being able to follow directions but not lead, place her or him in an activity that has a leader in charge. Make sure that the leader understands that her or his volunteers may need a great deal of prodding and reminding.

Most followers are reliable worker bees. They're the ones who pick up the flowers, assemble the press kits and go with someone on the ask. They deserve to be thanked beautifully for the work they do.

My favorite worker bee thanking strategy is that of my associate, Beverly Galley. When she produced a very large auction in Marin County, she was always careful to pull really awful items out of the cataloging process so that the tables would not look tacky. Instead of tossing the truly awful jewelry, plaster statues, plastic flower arrangements, she put them aside and used them as "awards" for the volunteers at the post-Auction volunteer party. Prizes would be given for soliciting the most items, landing the single best (or worst) item, and so on. One year they received a case of santa-dolls-on-bicycles that

What is your price?

...this all can come back to haunt you

ride in a circle and ring an obnoxious bell. She gave one of those treasures to her best worker bee. And even after that woman had stopped volunteering with the Auction and moved out of Marin, Beverly sent her a santa doll every year to remind her of the Auction and the esteem they held for her.

(Of course, this can all come back to haunt: nearly every "winner" re-donated his or her "prize" to the next Auction; and when Beverly left the Auction, guess what they gave her as a going-away present!)

I like volunteer recognition parties. They can be formal or informal — a gathering in the office, an annual volunteer recognition luncheon, whatever. One volunteer rule that may not be broken is: always write thank you notes (hand-done, personal as well as the formal ones from the Board) to your volunteers. Always thank them publicly — in your newsletter and/or a display ad in your local newspaper. And always give them a small memento to remind them of your organization and appreciation.

And don't forget the supreme compliment: invite your great volunteers to join up again!

LEADERS. In addition to warm formal and informal letters, mementos, and public kudos, thank your True Leader volunteers personally — at a Board meeting, your Annual Meeting or Open House. Write and place a feature story on him or her in the local newspaper. Do something very special: arrange baby-sitting for their next night on the town; find an

Always thank them publicly.

Do something special: "It's the thought that counts."

Thanking Volunteers:
The Cookie Story
My friend Flo did a capital campaign for a museum and reached her goal, and had a volunteer Victory Party. She did not follow the rule that you are supposed to punish the innocent. She in fact praised everyone appropriately, giving better prizes to people who raised more money and who did more work. But she had one volunteer who truly distinguished himself. At the party, she called him up on

out-of-print book on their favorite subject; send them a framed photograph taken on the night of the party. It doesn't have to be expensive. Like our mothers said, "It's the thought that counts."

You may decide to ask your leaders to join the Board. Wouldn't it be nice to have a tried-and-true fundraising leader sign up?

It is always a supreme compliment to be offered a bigger job with more responsibility for next year's campaign. Don't worry about your leader-volunteers taking on too much. They're experienced and know how to say "no".

stage and gave him the greatest honor possible: to have noticed, written down, and publicly acknowledged everything he did. On top of that, during the verbal accolades, the museum staff filed by and piled a mountain of his favorite cookies – home baked – at his feet. Put a price tag on that one.

How to do a Bike-a-thon

A Bike-a-thon is a fundraising activity that includes people who pay to enter, people who pledge to support the bicyclists' efforts, and business sponsors. The advantages of using this kind of athletic activity to raise money are: 1) It can raise a great deal of money in communities where bicycling is very fashionable; 2) It is wholesome and, if done well, will reflect well on your organization's work; and 3) It is a win-win-win fundraising activity because the bicyclists get to do what they love to do, the business sponsors get their name linked with a great event, and the organization raises money. The disadvantage is only one, and has to do with a cherished fundraising axiom: never do an event that depends on dogs, children or the weather. In other words, just one little rain storm or run of 105-degree days could ruin all of your plans.

The first step in producing a Bike-a-thon is having a beautiful, appropriate route. The MS Society in California recently felt the heat from the community when they charted a lovely course for a Bike-a-thon in Monterey that some sore bicyclists later referred to as "x#!+/# alpine!" It is fine to have a challenging course, but it is very important to market it as such. I have a friend who rode in the AIDS Bike-a-thon last year. She was a novice bicyclist, but the promos promised that one need not be in great shape to finish the race. At the end, she begged to differ.

The route must be very scenic and safe. You will need permits and a great deal of political and legal cooperation. You will probably want to regulate traffic on streets to ensure the safety of the cyclists. Where is the prettiest part of your community? Perhaps you could hold the event in a part of town people do not usually get to see: on private roads or through restricted territory. If you are planning an off-road event, you can market it only to mountain bike riders. Thinking through every step of the route is crucial. It is such a specialized field that here in California there are fundraising firms that do nothing but plan the details of the route for you (for marathons, too). Make sure, if you are going to plan the route yourself, that you enlist a team of experienced bicyclists who have five or more Bike-a-thons under their belts to consult on the details.

In addition to the experts, you will need a virtual army of volunteers the day of the event. Some of the volunteer tasks will be: registration, starting line, providing water stops along the route, clocking riders and awarding of prizes. Most Bike-a-thons provide entertainment at the end of the route. Some feed their bicyclists, either at stations along the way or at the end. Most Bike-a-thons provide at least T-shirts, orange sections and juice. Others give free massages on the spot at the end of the ride, and hand out free bicycling paraphernalia like shoes, caps and gloves.

The most popular Bike-a-thons give potential entrants the choice of how far they want to ride. The Tour de San FRANCEcisco offers a 10, 15 or 20 mile course. This attracts all levels of cyclists.

If you want to try a Bike-a-thon, I recommend that you build in a substantial amount of hoopla. Giving the event a great twist gives the riders more fun, makes it an event that will attract more people every year, and could even make it newsworthy. You could take each person's picture as they cross the finish line and, according to their number, have it available to take with them when they leave. Or you could have a mini-Bike-a-thon for children going on simultaneously. Or you could recruit your local "celebrities" (news station weatherman, mayor, radio talk show host, etc.) to staff the water stops along the

route. You could have a theme for your Bike-a-thon, like healthy hearts, with heart-shaped decorations, and a health fair at the end of the route with free blood pressure screening, chiropractic exams and cholesterol testing. You might try ending the ride with the world's largest Slip and Slide – off their bikes and down a wet, plastic-covered hill into a pool.

Marketing for such an event is fairly straightforward. Although you will want to advertise in the local media to pick up people who do not usually enter such events, the bulk of your advertising budget will go to purchasing lists of people who enter other Bike-a-thons. You should consider leafletting bicycle clubs and bike stores. Happily, the people who join Bike-a-thons are fairly easy to find. In order to attract them, the entry fee should be competitive, and the little extras you provide (beautiful route, free food, etc.) should be explained in detail.

A Bike-a-thon is a good opportunity for advocacy groups to raise money because it does not matter if the entrants believe in you or not. You are not asking for agreement on the issues you are addressing. You are asking people who like to ride bicycles to come enjoy a day in the sun. The fun details of the event are marketed, and who it benefits is always secondary unless you have an extremely popular issue right now. The aforementioned AIDS Bike-a-thon benefits a very popular issue, so the cause gets as much press as does the race. But this is the exception, not the rule.

A WORD OF CAUTION: There is a trend right now in some Bike-a-Thons to require that every rider pay a fairly hefty fee to enter and raise a large minimum in pledges. Although the organization's net take from the event will probably stay the same or grow for several years, I believe that this trend could eventually make the famous "How to Lose Donors Like Crazy" list. There is some competition for bicyclists, and they will avoid the Bike-a-thons that are too expensive and/or demanding and flock toward the fun, challenging, inexpensive ones. The organization that makes its Bike-a-thon better every year, not more expensive, will be the one to see the event become traditional and provide reliable yearly income.

CHAPTER FIFTEEN
Working With Foundations

What Are They, Anyway?

A Foundation is a tax-exempt organization set up to give money away. Some foundations are set up by a person or family with money to take a more organized approach to requests for assistance. Some foundations are set up to raise money in a community and distribute it to community-identified non-profits. And some foundations are established by corporations to manage the requests they receive for assistance from non-profits. Some foundations are staffed, which could mean one person who answers the phone or a full complement of experts, each of whom specializes in one particular kind of non-profit. Some foundations are not staffed, which means that you could send them a request for money and receive a "no", cut and dried, by return mail, or never hear back at all, and never really know what happened.

Generally, foundations begin with a pot of money to be invested, with the income generated to be given away. Alternately, some corporate foundations give money annually instead of tying up the corpus; the amount depends on profits from the previous year. The way that a corporate foundation is funded is actually important to know because you can count on one that is endowed, like Packard Foundation, to give steadily no matter how the Hewlett Packard stock is doing, whereas a foundation like Chevron's, funded year to year with corporate contributions, has gone seriously up and down according to gas prices and refinery problems. At this writing the Chevron Foundation, once a mighty bastion of enlightened giving, has virtually shut down.

First the foundation identifies and sets aside the money, then it develops the criteria for giving it away. This rule also has its exceptions, those being the newer, very idealistic foundations formed to rectify imbalances in traditional kinds of funding. The Women's Foundation in San Francisco is one example. That foundation was started by a handful of women with relatively limited means who decided that funding for women's and girls' programs in the Bay Area had received the short end of the stick long enough. They formed the Foundation based on this vision, raised the money, at first nickel by dime, with a first year goal of $200,000. By the way, it is interesting to note that they plucked that figure from the sky. $100,000 seemed too low, but $300,000 seemed too high. They came within $3,000 of their goal the first year, and they had no real program to sell because they had not yet given a grant. So for them, first came the vision, then came the money, then came the structure. However, usually for foundations first comes the money, then comes the structure; but sometimes the vision never comes at all. If you have experience with foundations that give only to their Board members' (constantly changing) pet projects, you know that all giving isn't focused and/or enlightened.

You can learn about all of the various foundations at your local funding library. If you are not sure where that might be, try giving your local public library a call. Many communities have regional funding libraries available for free where you can take an orientation training from their staff and then work on your own to research which foundations have your particular cause within their field of interest.

So You Want to Get a Grant

For many non-profits with little experience in fundraising, getting a grant looks like the easiest, most lucrative way to get started. The money is just sitting there to be asked for! But there are several problems with using foundation grant-writing as your primary fundraising strategy:

1) Of all of the money given in a single year by corporations, individuals, foundations and through bequests, foundation giving accounts for only approximately 5%. Corporate giving is another 5%, gifts through bequests are another 10%, and individual giving accounts for the remaining 80%. Foundations are not where the money is.

2) Foundations like to fund new, start-up programs or special projects within your organization. By and large, they will not give large amounts for on-going operating costs. And if they do fund a project, they want to know where the money will come from in subsequent years, because it will not be coming from them.

3) The current success rate for grants is approximately 7%. That

How To Lose Donors Like Crazy

Tip #7: *Write a proposal asking for $100,000 for operating expenses, mimeograph it and send it to every foundation in the directory.*

means that 93% of all requests to foundations are turned down. The primary reason for this is what we call the "shotgun approach" that non-profits take to grant writing. They xerox the research book, write the "definitive grant" asking for $50,000, copy it and send it to every foundation in the book. Wrong. Research, matching the foundation to your mission and geographic area, is the key. If you come away from a research session with three very possible matches, you've spent your time well. Each request must be tailored to the particular focus of each foundation you are approaching.

4) The longer you rely on grants and ignore building your base of individual donors, the more project-oriented and dependent you will be. I worked with an organization in San Francisco that started primarily as a counseling center. They started with grants, and had a director who was very influential locally and able to attract them from government and foundations. Money became available for a senior program, so she opened a Senior Center in the basement. Suddenly they were bursting at the seams. The original counseling center was hurting for money, and the new program was doing fine for awhile. Eventually, the senior monies dried up. Then money came available for drug and alcohol counseling. Money is money, right? So she went for it, and got it. While the center itself was seemingly bursting with life and activity, the central programs, the ones at the heart of their real mission, were suffocating for lack of money and space. This strategy for survival, based on grants, allows the grant-makers to design your programs based on their values and whims, not your vision and mission.

...the "shotgun" approach to grant writing

Research is the key.

Good research takes time, and is on-going. It does not make sense to buy books that tell you which foundations give where unless you are a very large organization whose budget comes, to a large degree, from foundations because that information changes very often. It is a more cost-effective strategy for most organizations to create a form that can be used to collect data and schedule regular trips to the funding library for research sessions.

...good research takes time

Grant Writing

Grant writing is unnecessarily mystified. Every foundation requires a slightly different approach, so read the guidelines and **follow** them. If they want a cover letter or letter of intent, that is a short, 1 and 1/2 page piece explaining what your organization does, what you want to do, how much it will cost, and how you want the Foundation to participate. The "grant", usually a longer version of the cover letter, may ask for your mission, a list of your Board members **and** their financial commitment to the project, a financial statement, and other documents. If you have a good long range plan, and if you produce regular financial statements and are audited yearly, you will be able to put together the documentation for the grant. The grant itself is PROSE. That means that you must describe your organization's work in human terms and paint a realistic, vivid, understandable, exciting, human picture of what you want to do with the money you are requesting. For those of us who cut our grant writing teeth on government requests, this can be

Read the guidelines and follow them.

Paint a realistic, vivid, human picture of what you want to do.

237

difficult. Let me suggest the following vocabulary list:

INSTEAD OF...	USE...
Units of service	patients in our Clinic
multiservice organization	community center designed to help our neighbors solve landlord disputes & mediate with employers for their rights
fiscally sound	for seven consecutive years, operating within our projected budget
at risk	babies whose teenaged mothers abused drugs during pregnancy
learning disabled	people who look at this page of words and see a jumble of letters
emotionally disturbed	teenagers who have been violently abused and left to figure out life on their own

frail elderly	people over 65 whose bones are brittle and break easily, and who are afraid of falling, and not having anyone to help them back up
juvenile offenders	children who drift away from positive to negative role models and smash up against the law
civil rights	the American standard that the freedoms provided for in the Constitution were meant for all
horticultural therapy	teaching disabled people how to make seeds turn into flowers, and planting in those people seeds of self-worth and hope.

Before you venture into pursuing foundations, I encourage you to make a list of "buzz words" like the ones in the left column above that you use to describe what you do. It is true that shorthand like "civil rights" has its importance. You need to use abbreviations when you talk to people who know what your work is about, like other social workers, health care workers or advocates. But when you are making a request to a foundation for funding, make absolutely sure that you reinforce the shorthand with descriptive phrases like the ones in the right hand column above. Do not presume that funders understand the importance of what you do! One of my favorite foundation staff people came to his job with no background in health care, which was to be his area of "specialty", nor did he know much about fundraising. He is smart and quick enough to get out in the field and learn, but I am quite sure that requests that explain the importance of the work being done are more moving, readable and memorable to him than ones filled with health care jargon.

There are classes offered on grant writing in most communities. A trainer myself, I am a strong advocate for fundraisers getting as much training as they can, so I urge you to consider attending one of these classes. For folks who write grants all the time, the classes give you a chance to get feedback and serve as a refresher and motivator. For novices, having a class under your belt will increase your confidence and encourage you to go try your hand at getting a grant.

Is Responding to Requests Enough?

We have looked at Foundations through the grant seeker's glasses. Now let's pull back and take a more global look at the process.

A pot of money exists to be invested and the income will be

Do not presume that funders understand the importance of what you do.

240

given away to non-profits that meet certain criteria. Staff is hired to review the grant requests and make recommendations for funding to the Board. The staff will also go out into the field and see performances, visit clinics and attend non-profit conferences to stay familiar with the quality of the non-profits in the community. Criteria and guidelines are drawn up based on the values of the people who provide the money and will make the funding decisions, and the convenience of the staff to process the requests.

The non-profit sends a staff person to the funding library to research grants. The criteria of several hundred foundations are scanned to make a match with their mission, and notes are taken about how to apply and what particular area the foundation likes best: youth, mentally ill, cancer, research, performing arts, etc. The guidelines are xeroxed and brought back to the office, where a request is prepared that speaks to the foundation's priorities. The staff person connects with the foundation staff to advise them of the grant that is being sent, and the foundation staff encourages them to apply but offers little hope that it will be funded because, "Money is very tight this quarter." The request is mailed, its existence is reported to the Board, and everyone at the non-profit crosses their fingers that it will be funded.

Whose needs are being met by this process? Actually, the answer is fairly broad. The needs of the foundation staff to have a job and get the job done as easily as possible are being met. But in the process staff often feel hounded and unappreciated

Whose needs are met?

241

by the non-profit community that does not understand how difficult it is to have to continually say no. Foundation staffs sometimes become defensive, trying to protect themselves from attack from the community, although it is really a Board that makes up the criteria and decides who gets the money. This defensiveness could be misconstrued in the non-profit community as aloofness at best, hostility at worst.

The need of the foundation's Board is being met. They are often taking someone else's money and giving it away, thereby giving themselves a sense of being philanthropic and bountiful. But often the organizations that they fund in good faith have not revealed what dire straits they are in and the grant that they receive winds up being good money thrown after bad. The organization flounders, struggles and gives up the ghost, and the foundation feels ripped off. A program executive at the San Francisco Foundation tells a story of a large non-profit that was awarded a very large grant. They seemed stable and solid. But several months later they returned, saying that they needed another huge grant to avoid closing their doors. Months before, they had concealed one small detail: they were running so far in the red that the first large grant could not save them. The Foundation staff member and the Board felt betrayed. They withheld the second grant and the organization folded.

Foundation grants **seem** to be meeting the need of the non-profit for funding. After all, no one is twisting the arm of the non-profit to request the money for the project that they insist they really want to do. But unless the project money meets an urgent and central need for the non-profit, the real need of the organization to fulfill its mission is not being met.

The most important need is often not examined: Is the grant meeting the need of the community? "Need" in the non-profit world is often misunderstood. Organizations have no need. If they need to make payroll, or if they need money to paint scenery, print flyers, buy a new microscope, or put gas in the van, that's their Board's problem. "Need" in the truest sense for non-profits means: What does the community need? What need are we entrusted by our non-profit status to meet, and is the need being met by this grant?

Organizations do not have "needs".

In order to determine if the most important need is being met, start by examining why your organization exists. What human needs are you trying to meet? If you are a local opera company, you exist to bring opera to your community, you serve as a developer and refiner of local talent, often sending the best and the brightest off to more glittering stages, and you take opera into the schools to educate children about the medium. A grant request to fund a liaison between your company and the schools makes sense. A grant request for money to hire a firm to conduct a national advertising campaign does not.

When foundations provide funding opportunities for very specific projects, it can be tempting to apply. "Money is money," they say in non-profits. "Let's go for it!" A non-profit manager in the Bay Area called recently to pursue hiring me to conduct a feasibility study for fundraising strategies. It finally turned out

"Money is money. Let's go for it."

243

that he wanted to "go after" a grant providing fundraising technical assistance - although they didn't really need to raise money! He thought it would be a good "in" for his organization with the funder.

But why should the non-profit organization have to start with the foundation's criteria and try to fit itself into it like trying on the glass slipper? Pulled back as we are to look at the bigger picture, suppose another model existed. Suppose foundations took a different approach to funding, and each foundation targeted one community (large or small) problem (large or small) to solve. Suppose The X Foundation targeted illiteracy for the coming three years. Rather than having everyone scrambling to find a way to make illiteracy a part of their program (reading operatic scores to adults who don't read?), The X Foundation would propose a five-part approach to ending illiteracy:

1) Money to buy books geared to adult interest with levels of proficiency outlined;

2) Money to train volunteer teachers;

3) Advertising money to recruit volunteers;

4) Incentive monies for inner city schools with the highest reading score improvements;

5) Production money for video tapes to introduce illiterate adults to the joys of reading.

And what if The X Foundation then targeted all of the organizations already doing this kind of work and asked for

...trying on the glass slipper

their most inventive and cost-effective way to meet these five criteria? Or suppose they convened a think tank of the best and the brightest in all fields relating to illiteracy? An educational publishing firm may have the perfect solution to creating the books, the local volunteer bureau already has the skills to recruit and screen the volunteers and seventeen great ideas for an advertising campaign, the PTA's might apply to develop the incentive program in the schools, and the local alliance of non-profit media might be set up to create the videos. Or perhaps it might turn out that the people who have been turning out alternative textbooks have a better approach to the reading materials. And the neighborhood free clinic, already in the habit of recruiting and screening volunteers, may have a more innovative approach to the recruitment problems. How about getting the teachers union to work on an incentives program? And perhaps the TV station in the closest big city would produce and distribute the video tapes for free.

What I am outlining is called pro-active funding. This means, rather than funding projects that non-profits have to invent, foundations would take the lead in identifying community needs that already meet the areas of interest for the foundation and enter into a partnership with non-profits to meet those needs in the most efficient and effective ways possible. It requires more time and effort from the foundations' Board and staff. But the only really important need to be met by foundation funding is the need of the community, and this model works better than the one now being widely followed. I also believe, in the long run, that it would be more rewarding to the

...the only really important need to be met by the foundation funding is the need of the community

foundation staffs and would be more exciting and challenging for the non-profits as well.

Vision and Control

What is the foundation world's responsibility to excellence? If they identify a problem and throw some money at it, are they doing their job? If need exists in the community, and a non-profit steps forward to meet that need, how much can a foundation or any funding source interfere in the carrying out of the mission? The issue is control vs vision.

"Vision" on the part of the foundation means setting out to solve a problem or meet a need and building coalitions to make the solution possible. It means listening to the community about what the problem really is, and collaborating with the non-profits that have as their mission solving pieces of that puzzle. It means staying focused on the big picture and investing foundation money where it will do the absolute most good: not in the biggest or flashiest organization, not in the organizations that lobby the best for the money, not in the pet project of the chairman, but in the organizations that best address the need.

"Control" means using the funding to blackmail a non-profit into doing business the way that the funding source wants business done. In some communities, United Way has demanded that the non-profits that they fund create

It means staying focused on where the money will do the most good.

I once worked with an arts organization that had been told by its primary foundation funding source that their grant for the year was being withheld until the organization put together a better-functioning Board, and they gave the group money to hire a consultant to help them do just that. When I came to this organization, five or six of the performers, along with their spouses, were Board members and they spent Board meeting time

246

programming as United Way thinks it should be created, threatening to withhold money if the organization does not comply.

Ideally, every non-profit needs a functioning Board. It is very difficult to make it in this rough world without some folks who will help you to keep your perspective and bring you in some money, which is what a good Board does. But there are better ways to convey this message, and similar suggestions concerning better ways to operate, than blackmail:

❖ Education. Foundations in general spend a great deal of energy educating non-profits on how to apply for money. How about providing free, non-judgmental seminars on how to become excellent organizations?

❖ Rewarding excellent models. It might inspire other non-profits if foundations set aside some money to award to non-profits that develop superior operational strategies. Such a program could be modeled after the famous "genius" awards that are given to individuals who demonstrate innovative ways to address the problems of humanity.

❖ Partnership. Foundations often build in ways to prevent their staff and Board from interacting with non-profits. Citing "conflict of interest", membership on the Boards of non-profits is usually discouraged. I challenge this model. In addition to giving money, foundation personnel have tremendous opportunities to network and share information with all of the non-profits in their communities. By making foundation staff and volunteers available to non-profits to build coalitions and

talking about how tall the risers should be and what color skirts they would wear for the next performance. They smiled at me and listened as I talked about how a real Board could help them to raise money and do the planning they needed to do if they wanted to remain a viable part of the arts community in the Bay Area. We brainstormed some names of possible Board members, but week after week it turned out that they were just too busy to make their calls to these people. Finally I figured it out: they did not want a Board. They were going through the motions because the foundation had insisted that they do so. I went to them with an ultimatum: if they truly did not want a Board, say so and I would go to the foundation myself and explain that their rules could not be superimposed on this group. But if they wanted to try having a policy-making and money-raising

247

work together to strengthen community, some of the imbalances of power that now exist between foundations and the organizations they fund would begin to break down. Non-profits would have no reason not to tell the truth to potential funding sources. "The truth" would actually be the heart of the problem that the foundation could be intervening to help solve. If foundations had a stake in meeting community need rather than existing to throw money at community problems, the needs would begin to be met.

Evaluation of Success

The one word on a grant application that makes non-profit managers scratch their heads most is "evaluation". How will you evaluate the success of this project? Most grant writers line up the typewriter and type in, "The objective of this project is to increase participation. The goal is to have more participation. We will know it was a success if there is more participation."

The evaluation part of any project is, in fact, a wonderful opportunity for your organization to check in with the community and make sure that you really are meeting a need. Set the foundation's rules aside and grab hold of the great opportunity "evaluation" has to offer.

Most organizations start with a vision and create some ways to make their vision a reality. So you want to turn your uncle's barn into a musical showcase for local talent. Great! Get the

"The objective of this project is to increase participation. The goal is to have more participation. We will know it was a success if there is more participation."

barn, get some money, some lumber, new windows, comfortable seats, lights, a sound system, musicians, scripts, singers and dancers, and away you go. The first play is exciting. The second more difficult. You are distracted because the performers want more money. The roof leaks. You look up and it's three years later. How do you know that you are meeting a community need? If you believe that the numbers of tickets you are selling is the answer, I urge you to re-consider.

If your organization is a 501(c)(3) you have an obligation as a citizen of the community you are serving to make that community a better place. This is the most misunderstood aspect of non-profit status, and it is the central thesis of this book. If society gives you dispensation from taxes, that is because you are performing a service that the community needs. Notice that I am not saying audience needs, or patient needs, but community. In order to make sure that you continue to be relevant to your community, I suggest that you stop what you are doing every three years or so and get out into the community and find out if you are really meeting a need. What can an arts organization do for the community besides sing and dance? You can:

❖ educate children about the arts

❖ educate local politicians on the importance of the arts in the community

❖ network with other arts organizations to make sure that they are all relevant, efficient and of the highest quality

❖ serve on other non-profit Boards to make sure that the arts are

Stop what you are doing, every three years or so, and get out into the community...

present in medical, foundation, environmental and all consciousnesses, and not just an afterthought
❖ teach classes at the local junior college
❖ encourage young artists with auditions, talent contests and scholarships

Staying in your barn and singing your songs seems like the right thing to do. It is your mission. People pay money to see it. But what if one day people stop coming? When the seats in your barn are empty, it is too late to begin educating the community, or screaming at the world, that your medium is wonderful. If the next generation grows up without the arts being a major presence in their lives, your organization and every other arts endeavor will be in big trouble because that generation of people will not even think to buy a ticket to a live show. Tell them now why the arts are more exciting than their VCR's. Show them! Let them feel the vibrations that rise up from the soles of your feet when the audience starts clapping. All it takes is getting out into your community to find out what the people need.

...to find out what the people need.

What can the local day care center do for the community? Of course, your job day in and day out is to be there to take care of the community's children. And if you are non-profit, chances are that you are low-cost, over-worked and under-paid. But other than your stated mission, what are the boundaries of your citizenship in the community? You can:
❖ lobby for day care in corporations and with politicians

❖ create networking systems with perinatal providers to stay up-to-date on what problems the next generation of children will be facing (low birth weight, fetal alcohol syndrome, addiction, etc.) and help educate pregnant women about the dangers

❖ serve on local PTA Boards to make sure that your little clients are being prepared for life in the real world at school

❖ take the children on talk shows to educate the public on the wonderful job day care centers are doing, as opposed to the often harsh criticism they receive as poor substitutes for mom at best, abusers at worst

❖ provide respite emergency care for out-of-home working mothers who have no place to leave their child with 20 minutes notice

❖ provide children's art for local festivals

❖ take the children to local rest homes to visit the elders

These are not shopping lists that should be taken as a challenge to your organization. Rather they are some ideas of how the non-profit can interface with the community within the boundaries of its mission, and live up to its role as a citizen of the community it serves. Doing your job every day is not only not enough, it's not even a good idea. Too many non-profits put their nose to the grindstone, complaining every day about how hard it is to just survive, but by the time they stop to take a breath and look up and out into the community, they are obsolete. Even if you have a viable service, you're charging enough to make a living and you have three or four "reliable"

Doing your job every day is not only not enough, it's not even a good idea.

251

funding sources, it is still imperative to get out into the community and listen to people's needs. If you are not meeting real community needs, you are not living up to your obligation as a 501(c)(3).

The best way to begin to assess community needs is to get out and talk to the people who care about your issue. If you are a battered women's shelter, in order to make sure that you are the absolute best that you can be and to insure that you are doing everything you can about battering within your community, you might go out and talk to:
   -former clients, their supportive families and friends
   -the police
   -other shelters in other communities
   -teachers
   -organizations working with abused children
   -lawyers working with temporary restraining orders
   -judges
   -the media
   -employers
   -insurance companies
   -re-entry college programs

Find out what they think about your program, what they know about the issues, and what they think should be done about battering in your community. Listen and take notes.

The moaning is perceptible even from this distance: "We don't have time to do all of this!" I say to you, it is not about time. It

There is never any extra time.

is about priorities. We all have the same 24 hours in our day. In order to do the evaluation, the fundraising, the PR, the volunteer recruitment and thanking, and do it all well, you will have to put some other things on hold. Or at least put them on the back burner. Or make a giant leap and hire another person to help carry the load. The community interface is not an "extra" to be gotten to when there's extra time. There never is any extra time. Start now.

Foundations and the Community

We have looked at the evaluation process as an opportunity for the non-profit organization to take the temperature in the community and find their very important niche. And we have looked at how the foundation and the non-profit might create coalitions to address real community needs. But, setting the non-profit organization aside, what is the relationship of the foundation with the community?

Once again, it is true that society's stamp of approval making a foundation tax-exempt means that the foundation has a responsibility to society, to the community it serves, to solve some problems or meet some needs. But foundations, especially "Community" foundations, face the same problem as 501(c)(3) non-profits do: the word Community often means to a foundation that they are expected to raise money from the community, and that's where the relationship ends. The responsibility that comes with their relationship to the community they serve is as obscure as it usually is for a non-profit within a community.

Foundations spin in a world populated with requests, meetings, guidelines and deadlines. The foundation staffs go to conferences and talk to other funders and talk constantly in person and on the telephone to non-profits trying to get money from them. Some foundations go to the corporate parent for money, some go to the community to raise money. Most foundations have hand-picked people sit on their Boards. These people are usually prestigious, some are major donors themselves, and they filter the information given to them by the staff, apply the criteria and approve or disapprove grants.

For most foundations, there is a large piece missing. Where is the community? They are, hopefully, at the bottom of the money tube, getting the services that the foundation is funding. But they are very rarely at the top of the process ladder, giving input to the foundation powers about where the money should be invested. Again, like the non-profits they fund, foundations have a backwards notion of where the community "fits" in their work. The community exists, for foundations, to get the services that the non-profits provide, but most foundations seem to be too close to the forest to see the trees. The ONLY important factor in this entire equation is whether or not the money they are spending is helping the community in some way. Rarely does a foundation get out into the community to see if their grants are having a real impact. Is the problem being solved? Is the need being met? They too often rely on non-

...a world populated with requests, meetings, guidelines and deadlines

Everything is running smoothly, all deadlines are being met, and people are still starving in the streets.

profit after-the-fact reports to assess their effectiveness. And then too often the "impact" that is of utmost concern to funders and non-profits alike is the "impact" that the grant had on the smooth functioning of the non-profit. So in the meantime, everything is running smoothly, all deadlines are being met, payrolls made, the foundation Board is satisfied with themselves, and people are still starving in the streets.

One of the finer foundations in terms of accountability is The Packard Foundation. Nancy Glaze, who is in charge of the arts funding, really takes the time to get into the schools and see the progress being made with Packard funding. In fact, they are so in tune with their responsibility to the community that they are sending Nancy across the country to observe a public school that serves a low income community. That particular school has an outstanding arts program and Packard might like to use it as a model that they would fund elsewhere.

In order for foundations to take their rightful place as citizens of their communities, whether they are community foundations or any other color or hue, it is essential that staff get out from behind their desks and go talk to the people they plan to fund. They must understand the problems and issues, and they must monitor not only the disbursement of funds, but the movement of progress as well. They must take responsibility for spending the money, no matter whose money it is, in the most effective way if they are to deserve the honor of tax-exempt status in this society.

How to Approach a Foundation

Which is the correct approach?

A) Take off your hat, and hold onto it as you drop to your knees and crawl

B) Before applying, call them up and tell them that your daddy is President and you won't take no guff

C) Copy 100 pages from the appropriate Directory in the funding library, mimeograph three or four hundred requests that all begin "To Whom It May Concern" and mail them out bulk rate to save money.

If the truth be known, all three have been tried and are probably being tried again as you read this page. Foundation grant writing is usually the very first strategy adopted by a fledgling non-profit, so the first attempts tend to be a bit haphazard.

The best way to approach a Foundation is to begin with exhaustive research. Start with your local funding library, writing down everything that you can about what they fund, how much their average grant is, how to approach them, and who else they fund. But do not stop there. There is much more work to be done before you approach a foundation for the first time.

If you are acquainted with some of the other organizations the foundation funds, call them up and find out everything that you can about how the foundation works and how they managed to get their grant approved.

When you have found out everything you can from outside sources, go to the horse's mouth if you can. If the foundation is staffed and open to receiving phone calls, by all means call them. Tell them what you have in mind and see if it sounds fundable. Even better, go to see them if you can. It is simply human nature that we trust people more if we can look them in the eye and size them up. Let the funders see what a respectable, down-to-earth good person you are. (If you look shifty, send someone else.)

If the foundation has guidelines, follow them. I know that this sounds simple, but too often it is overlooked. Read the guidelines and send them what they want. Do not make the foundation staff call you for the By-Laws. If By-Laws are requested, send them.

I have heard foundation staff people say that the actual presentation of the grant is not important: "It could be written on toilet paper," they claim. That may be true, but as a teacher who has to read twenty hand-written mid-terms at a time and grade twenty final projects, I guarantee that a fine, well-thought out presentation makes a difference. It should be pleasant to look at in color and have some photographs or art work. It must be readable and tell your story from a human perspective. It must make a great argument not only for needing the money, but for your ability to spend it well. However, it must not be too slick. When applying to a foundation, avoid the following:

❖ video tapes, unless requested. It makes you look rich. The arts may send videos, but please let the staff know if you want them back and where to send them.

❖ tiny print. Remember that these folks have to read through hundreds of requests at a time. Have mercy on their tired eyes.

❖ spelling errors... especially misspelling the name of the foundation, or its Executive Director (it happens!)

❖ illegible IRS letter. Yes, they must be able to read it.

❖ confusing financial data. Please clearly delineate how much you earned last year, where the money came from, and where you spent it.

❖ too many words.

❖ assuming that they know what you do. Spell out what services or performances you gave last year and what you intend to do this year.

❖ trying to make it sound like more than it is. A bandaid is all right when it's a bandaid that's called for. If it's a bandaid, do not try to make it sound like brain surgery.

❖ trying to take a need for operating monies and make it sound like a new and exciting project. If the foundation funds only projects and you do not have a project, go somewhere else for money.

❖ hiding the request. Nancy Glaze at Packard finds this to be the most frustrating element of having to read through grants. She recommends an extremely clear cover letter

A word about "competition" here. If you are shaking your head "no" at my suggestion that you call other non-profits for information because you believe that you could never get that kind of information from another non-profit because you are in competition for the money, I want you to know that the relationship any non-profit has with a foundation has a life of its own. It is not possible to "steal" a foundation funder from another non-profit. Other non-profits will find out that the foundation exists just as you did and they will make their own approach. Chances are that the grant a non-profit gets will be the only one they ever get from that foundation. If they get others in succeeding years, it is because of the good work they are doing. Also, the money given to another non-profit is not the last grant out the door. There is more money in there to be had by other

stating who you are, what you do, what you want from them and the amount of money being requested.

Finally, remember to thank them. Keep them on your mailing list and invite them to special events. Send them your wonderful newsletter. If the foundation receives an award or gets a good write-up in a newspaper or fundraising journal, send them a note. In other words, treat the foundations that give you money like major donors. They are.

non-profits. And in my experience, any non-profit fundraiser who refuses to give you information about his or her own strategies for successful fundraising probably is a charlatan. The really good fundraisers share their ideas. Some even share the names of donors that they think would be amenable to your cause. Do not be afraid to ask.

CHAPTER SIXTEEN
Working With Corporations

In the early 1980's, President Reagan announced that the federal government was getting out of the charity business, cutting non-profits from the national budget and agenda. He said that he "hoped" that the corporate sector would step in and step up their giving. In fact, the feds encourage corporations to give by allowing them to donate up to 10% of their pre-taxed earning to non-profits and write it off.

There was a small surge of hope back then that corporations would rise to the occasion. But we all know that they did not. In fact, according to *Giving USA*, corporate giving fell in 1988 for the first time ever. What's going on?

Attitude

Set aside the huge topic of CORPORATE GIVING and look for a moment at the people behind the labels. First, how do non-profit people feel about corporate people? Our attitudes set the stage for the relationship. As I travel and teach, the topic of corporate giving often comes up. Why aren't they giving more? So I ask this group of kind, loving non-profit folks, "what comes to mind when I say corporation?" The list usually looks something like this:

-three piece suit

-can't get through the secretary
-only care about profits
-arrogant
-glass towers
-where the money is
-racist, sexist, homophobic
-untouchable

While this exercise is taking place, my sweet non-profit folks have turned into an angry mob, remembering every encounter they've had with those corporate types, and getting ready to do battle. Then I ask, "If this were a room full of corporate executives, and I asked what comes to mind when I say 'non-profit worker', what would **they** say?" They laugh nervously and respond with a list that usually looks like this:

-bleeding heart
-can't make it in the for-profit world
-poor managers
-aging hippies
-always have their hands out
-unrealistic

I would say that both lists are true. The sides are lined up facing each other, Birkenstock to wing tip, and they don't understand each other at all. They speak different languages and have seemingly different values. But they need each other desperately, and there's a way to create the dialogue that will lead to partnership.

Non-profits know that they need corporations and corporate people. They need their money and expertise. It is up to the non-profits to make the first move in this courtship, signal their willingness to get to know the corporate climate and way of doing things.

So first comes an attitude adjustment. Behind all of the negative images non-profits have about for-profits are real people. They plant flowers in their gardens, yell at their kids and worry about earthquakes just like we do. They go to work just like we do. But once they get there, they have different motivations, and therein lies the difference. People who work for corporations are under pressure to make money for the corporation, the stock holders and themselves. But if the corporation they work for does not make money, they will be out of work. It's that simple.

...attitude adjustment

Partnership

We all know that very few non-profit workers make much money. As a matter of fact, other than survival instincts, money is usually the farthest thing from a non-profit worker's mind. What they care about is the passion of their work, the art and healing and advocacy and the difference they are making in the world.

When "head hunters" go out and lure the best and the brightest, part of what they are selling is US!

That is where the partnership comes in. For although the non-profit sector needs corporate sponsorship, I urge you to remember that the corporate sector needs the services non-

263

profits are providing. When "head hunters" go out from corporations to lure the best and the brightest to their corporation, think about what they are selling: great schools, low crime rate, best medical care, flourishing arts, clean rivers, hills to hike, etc. US! They need the community-based services that we provide to make their workers happy enough to settle in and stay put. The people who work in corporate America need us as well. We're the good part, the giving and caring part of society. And when they're done selling widgets and counting pennies, we provide them with the volunteer opportunities they need to feel like they're contributing and making a difference.

When the earthquake struck at 5:04 on October 17th, 1989, it transformed the Bay Area in more than just geological ways. At 5:03 we were all absorbed in our own life dramas: starting to get dinner ready, fighting the traffic to get home, turning on the World Series, wrapping up a project for the night. At 5:06 when the first shaking stopped, the first thing this community did was find who was suffering and help. My favorite story is of the man who lives near the Oakland freeway that collapsed, top deck onto lower deck. After he realized that he was physically okay, he ran and got a flashlight and his car jack and climbed up onto the precarious freeway to try and free people who were stuck. I saw a film clip on television of a woman in high heels, carrying a brief case, who ran to join a brigade of people carrying a hose down a street to fight a fire. My own circle of colleagues, all women who own their own businesses or women with a great deal of responsibility within a corporate structure, got together after the quake and shared the common experience

At 5:06, when the first shaking stopped, this community set immediately to find who needed help.

264

of how good it feels to "get outside of yourself" and do something for people in need. They took blankets, food and clothes to the Red Cross. They went to where the shelters were set up and volunteered. One woman who is a pilot participated in an air lift of food into a county that was cut off because the roads were ripped and twisted by the earthquake. Whatever was important before the earthquake became less important in the face of human need. The media were deluged with calls from people who wanted to help: "Where am I needed?" I encourage everyone to hold onto that feeling. You can step out of yourself every day, the human need is so great and on-going. And that enrichment that you feel when you give of yourself is what the non-profit sector has to give every day.

Non-profit and for-profit corporate workers have to start talking with each other about what we all need. The arts have made great strides in creating a dialogue with corporations. Corporate giving to the arts rises every year as corporate giving to social services falls. In part this is due to the fact that the arts are clean and pretty. The only controversy or political overtones to the arts are in the avant garde movements, and they do not tend to attract the corporate gifts. Corporations can give or underwrite performances and get their name in the program and the paper. The arts do not have much trepidation about accepting just about any kind of corporate gift, including allowing cigarette companies to put their names on touring groups of dancers. Health groups would have some explaining to do to their constituency if they took money from a company whose product is linked to cancer. And the arts understand

This is what the non-profit sector offers every day.

265

partnership. The "Patron" system for supporting the arts is centuries old. It is not only acceptable to have wealthy underwriting, it is tradition.

I recommend that non-profits begin by having an open, honest discussion about whether or not you want to go after corporate money. Some of the questions you might want to address are:

-Do we want to set up a partnership with corporations? If not, why not?

-What can we offer corporations in terms of exposure in return for their gift: program ad space? Their name on our vans?

-How do our work and the work of local for-profit businesses complement each other and offer natural linkages?

-Can we provide promotional opportunities to corporations without appearing to "sell out"?

What Do They Want?

This is probably the most important question for you to answer if you decide to engage in corporate solicitation. Understand that corporations are accustomed to business relationships that give and take. They are used to dealing with sales people who can present sixteen excellent reasons why they should do business together. And those sales people know exactly what's in it for the corporation before they ever walk in the door to make their pitch. If they're selling copy machines, they will

Sales people know exactly what's "in it" for the corporation before they even begin their pitch.

266

know what kind the corporation uses now, if the secretaries are happy with the machine, if the executives are happy with the quality of copies, and how much they're paying for maintenance. The sixteen reasons they present for why the corporation should now do business with their company have to do with meeting the need of the corporation.

I know that the concept of sales makes most non-profit types very nervous. This discomfort tends to complicate your possible relationship with the corporate world and I suggest that if you are uncomfortable with the concept of "selling" your work to corporations that you stick to raising money through other means. (See "How to Conduct a Bake Sale")

"What Do They Want?" or **need** is the question at hand. Some needs that you could meet by allowing corporations to give to your organization are:

1) Help clean up their act. When a corporation falls out of favor with the buying public, one strategy for proving that they're the good guys is to give a large, public gift. In order to counter their image as a company that discriminates in hiring, Coors Beer gives a great deal of money in the Hispanic community. And when Exxon isn't spilling oil all over Alaskan waters, they are convincing us through advertising that they spend a great deal of money to preserve animals and land in the wilderness. Closer to home, in my community a very popular mom-and-pop store closed and a huge chain moved in. To soothe the out-raged locals, the chain made a large public gift to local education.

One strategy for proving they are the good guys is to give a large, public gift.

267

In order to engage in this kind of relationship, you must first make sure that it is worth it to you. There are two very good, contradictory arguments to be made here. First is the argument that there's no such thing as tainted money. By doing the good work that you do you are in effect cleansing the money with important community work. The contradictory argument is that, if you "sell out", your donors will become discouraged and leave you. The more political your organization is, the more potent the latter argument becomes. Imagine, for instance, the National Organization for Women taking money from Penthouse Magazine. Explain that one to your donors. You could try argument #1, but I don't think it would work. And it would affect your future credibility as well with the public.

...the more political your organization, the more potent the argument

I am not trying to make a case for either taking or spurning questionable money. I am, however, making a case for being extremely deliberate with your decision in these matters. Talk about it. Develop a policy. I have seen more than one organization get into trouble when a large, politically questionable gift is offered, and the organization is split about whether to take it or not. Set the policy first, before any gift is solicited.

Set policy first, before any gift is solicited.

2) Promote them through special events. Whether "tainted" or "clean", corporate money is now being heavily invested in large, well-promoted special events. Called Cause-Related Marketing, this kind of relationship is also somewhat controversial. There are many non-profit watchers who believe that the partnership between corporation and non-profit should

268

be philanthropic rather than business-oriented.

If Cause-Related Marketing is for you, the key to making this link is in thinking out what you might have that is of promotional value, and then finding the exact right corporation to underwrite the event. What is the "exact right" corporation? Here are some possibilities:

-One whose mission is similar to yours: preventative medicine and a health club chain; day care and a toy manufacturer; teen center and running shoes.

-One with a promotional budget looking for something "different", something beyond ads in the newspaper or a booth at the local community fair. The competition in the for-profit sector is keen in some areas. If you could make a convincing case for the corporation linking with your non-profit, and the corporation reaping a larger marketing value because of the association, you might be able to get the underwriting.

There are two ways to find out which corporations are "in the market" for a special event to sponsor. One way is to have key corporate people on your Board or serving in an advisory capacity to you. By "key" I mean people who know other corporate people and keep their ears open. The other way is to keep **your** ears open. Network with other non-profits. I once had a client who managed to get a chic department store opening as a benefit because the local hospital turned down the offer. The two Directors of Development were friends and the hospital alerted her friend of the opportunity. (By the way, the hospital turned it down because they require at least $10,000 net from all such affairs.)

It is essential that you do your homework before you approach any corporation. This is easier said than done. Unless a corporation has a foundation, they do not have to report where they give their money. This makes research very difficult, especially in the area of making marketing links. I recommend that you do as much research as you can in places like the Foundation Center or other libraries. Then you will have to hit the streets. Rather than thinking of corporate research like you think of foundation research, think of it more like the research you have to do before you approach a major individual donor. Start playing "Who Do You Know?" Find out where your Board members, volunteers and major donors work. If you've targeted a particular corporation, go visit them. Get a copy of their internal newsletter, if possible. Find out who the rising stars are and make contact with them. Talk with other non-profits about who supports them and how to make the approach.

...do your homework

Getting the Gift

The best way to get a corporate gift is to have someone on the "inside" ask for it. This means that the best strategy is to have one of your volunteers or friends who works for the corporation walk the request in with her or his name on the cover letter. If you do not have a contact, a gift is a long shot. The cover letter on your request will say that the Executive Director will be calling the person in charge of giving (or marketing, advertising, etc.) next week for an appointment. Remember, face-to-face asking is the most effective. When you call, if you have something to show the corporate person, invite him or her out. Show off your day care center, your soup kitchen. If all you have is filing cabinets and desks, go to them with your scrap book of victories.

I once heard a corporate giving officer brag that his corporation did not even read the request until the fourth approach. They said "no" three times "to see what they're made of." The only way I can explain this is that these people are accustomed to dealing with sales people who are very persistant. They want to make sure that you want a relationship, not just a quick sale. In any case, please keep in mind when you are approaching a corporation that they operate with a different set of rules. You must be business-like and willing to wheel and deal.

"Wheel and deal" is a difficult concept for many non-profits. All I really mean by this is to breathe and think on your feet. If the corporation's giving has been decided well into next year, do not crumble in defeat (or at de feet). Take a longer look — if the answer is "Not now," that's not a "No." She says "Not now," you ask, "When?" If she says "Not that much money," that's not a "No." You ask "How much?" Listening and responding without feeling rejected is the first step in wheeling and dealing. I recommend that you have your organization join your local

Have someone on the "inside" ask for the gift.

...think on your feet

271

Chamber of Commerce. In most communities, that is where the business people do business. Their "mixers" are not singles looking for dates. They are chances to network with one another, meet the people you are having trouble making an appointment with, have a cup of coffee together and get to know each other — as equals. It is a wonderful opportunity for the representative of your organization to stand up and say the name of your non-profit and let the business community see that you look almost normal (no fringe at Chamber meetings). In some communities it is the Rotary, or one of the animal clubs (Elks, Lions, etc.) that serves this function. Happily, these clubs are opening up to women, so there is no excuse not to join.

If you are looking for "things", that is donations of stuff other than money, corporate solicitation might be just the right strategy. Corporations and businesses often redecorate, discarding their old desks, copy machines, filing cabinets, etc. There are also businesses that produce the "things" that you need: paint, computers, baby clothes, tables, couches, canned food, carpeting, etc. Many corporations are more willing to give you things than they are to give you money.

If you have a list of the things you need, I recommend that you produce a formalized wish list. This book would then serve as back-up for when you approach a corporation for money and they say no. You could then ask them to take a look at your book to see if there is anything there that they could give. It would also serve as your major document for approaching corporations that make the things you need. Make sure that the

These clubs are opening up to women, so there's no excuse not to join.

Produce a formal wish book.

book is attractive and easy to use.

Last but not least, it is important for you to realize that in addition to money and things, corporations and businesses have **time** to give. Many of the larger, more progressive corporations have Loaned Executive programs. Here in the Bay Area, we have Business Volunteers for the Arts, and programs that involve both Harvard and Stanford MBA graduates who are willing to be placed for technical assistance in non-profits of their choice. Some corporations like Xerox and Wells Fargo "release" professionals to volunteer, and keep them on payroll. You might even manage to get your Certified Public Audit donated. The emphasis for most of these loaned executive programs is time-limited, specific problem solving. But often it happens that the executive falls in love with your non-profit and winds up either on the Board or soliciting a gift from the parent company for you, or both.

Some of the tasks a loaned executive could perform are:
- assist with the long range plan
- solicit for the corporate campaign
- set up your fundraising software
- develop staff benefit packages.

Reality check:
YES, there are ways to form linkages with corporations,
BUT you must know someone who can open the corporate door for you.

YES, there is a lot of money out there,
BUT few corporations know how to give it. Last year (1989) corporate giving fell. And at its best, corporate giving has only accounted for approximately 5% of philanthropy nationally. They can give up to 10% of their pre-taxed earnings to non-profits, but their giving averages out to less than 2%. And very few (6%) give more than $500 at a time to any non-profit.

YES, the bigger companies give more, with 50 of the largest corporations comprising 50% of the total corporate philanthropic giving,
BUT, the trend we are seeing is in local giving. Corporations that give are looking in their own back yards for recipients.

YES, United Way raises a great deal of money in the corporate sector,
BUT, most of that comes from the workers, many of whom feel pressured by their supervisors to give. And United Way is still a very conservative force, giving money in the community to preserve the status quo, not to empower disenfranchised peoples.

YES, corporate giving to the arts is growing,
BUT so are the numbers of arts organizations out there. The corporate buck is looking for the biggest bang, and that still means that the bigger, more established arts groups who can splash the corporate name over their performances will continue to attract the most money.

Part III
Cause and Commitment

CHAPTER SEVENTEEN
The Board of Directors

Board Responsibilities: The "Big Five"

Do Boards **have** to do fundraising? This question comes pleadingly from the hearts of extremely reluctant Board members. Isn't there another model?

I ask in return, do you need money? If money is no problem for your organization, then why are you reading this book? If you need money, that is the Board's problem. If you create programs, hire staff and commit to buying toilet paper and copy machines without identifying where the money will come from, you're doing only half the job.

As Boards back away from their fundraising obligation, they usually thrash around looking for "another model". That means that they want other people to raise the money so that they can spend it. Sometimes this works. But usually it doesn't. The sooner your Board members understand the full scope of their responsibilities, put the team in place to carry out those responsibilities and get on with it, the sooner your organization will reach its prime.

"Do we have to raise money?"

Well, do you need money?

275

The Board of Directors of a non-profit organization is usually a special group of volunteers who sign on to guide that organization's development. They struggle with finances, policies and supervision. But mostly, it seems, they struggle with who they are and what it means to be a Board Member.

When a Board is functioning excellently, it enjoys **100% attendance** and **100% giving**, every member raises money, and they have a team spirit that challenges every member to perform to the absolute best of his or her ability. An excellent Board has committees that form to answer specific needs, get their work done, report back to the Board and dissolve – to go on to a new, exciting Board task. The excellent Board lives in the future, guiding the organization forward and empowering the professional staff (paid or unpaid) to handle the day-to-day operations. And the excellent Board gives quality thought to the issues of planning and Board regeneration. They thank each other, trust each other and each member gets to grow in the areas of leadership development and community relations.

When a Board is functioning excellently, every member raises money.

Getting to "excellence" requires taking one deliberate step at a time. It starts with the best possible mix of people and an understanding that serving on your Board is an honor and privilege. And it requires the Board members all understand their roles and responsibilities. So let's start by looking at the five areas of responsibility for the Board:

Serving on your Board is an honor and a privilege.

1) **They set policy.** By setting policy I mean taking a broad brush and making a stroke. They must answer the question:

what will happen for which people at what cost? Setting policy involves drawing the parameters within which the staff can work. The process starts with the Board responding to an expressed community need and deciding what the mission and goals of the organization are. They then look at the scope of the need within the community and decide how much they can accomplish. So if the need is for high quality, affordable ballet, the Board has several options. They can distribute video tapes of ballets to schools, nursing homes and community centers. Or they can import different ballet companies from around the world to their community theater. Or they can form their own company. Each option has advantages and disadvantages, and each has a unique price tag. Whichever option they choose, they must also accept responsibility for finding the money to pay for it. Once the "program" is decided, they then can create the parameters that we know as "policies": you may not operate with an unbalanced budget, you may not fire anyone unfairly, etc. Please note that "policies" does not include diddling with the details. It is not the Board's responsibility to count paper clips or units of long distance service, nor is it "policy" to write brochures by committee, hire line staff or negotiate copy machine contracts. If a Board member is invited by the Executive Director (paid or unpaid) to serve one of these detailed functions, the Board member takes off his or her Board hat, puts on his or her volunteer hat, serves the function and goes away.

Making policy does not include diddling with the details.

2) **They hire, and if necessary fire, the Executive Director** (paid or unpaid). I am including "paid or unpaid" in reference to the

Executive Director because organizations that are all-volunteer or have a Director who is not paid often get very confused about roles. The Executive Director, whether she or he receives a salary or not, serves at the pleasure of the Board. The Executive Director is the professional who sees to the day-to-day running of the organization and answers to the Board for the decisions he or she makes. Salary has nothing to do with this relationship. The Executive Director tends to the details, hires the other staff, and makes sure that the policies of the Board are carried out. If the Executive Director is not doing his or her job, the Board has the option to fire that person and find someone who will do a better job, but they do **not** have the option to go in and do it themselves. Some organizations, most notably arts groups, often have one person who sees to the business and one person who sees to the art. These two usually report separately to the Board concerning their fiefdoms. It is my fondest hope that some day the arts will see that "art" and "business" can be conceived and carried out by the same human being, and the separate directorships will become a thing of the past.

3) **They evaluate the organization.** This responsibility is often taken very lightly. Boards need to realize that they are legally responsible for the decisions made by them and their staff. Boards can get insurance to protect their personal property from being attached by angry debtors like the Federal government, but my concern here is not only legal but moral. The Board has the obligation to the community to know what is going on in the non-profit they are directing. When an organization makes ends meet by not paying their payroll taxes and they wind up

The Executive Director tends to the details, hires the other staff, and makes sure the policies of the Board are carried out.

It is not a good sign when the Board says, "We had no idea this was going on!"

278

on the front page of the newspaper, it is not a good sign when the Board President is quoted as saying, "We had no idea this was going on!"

Evaluation is much more than reading the Executive Director's report in Board meetings. It is much more than looking at the Treasurer's report and making sure that you're not spending too much on paper clips. Evaluation means teaching every Board member what the organization is supposed to be doing, showing them what the books look like, and giving them a chance to see for themselves. I recommend that organizations have rotating evaluation teams that go into the organization quarterly, talk with the Executive Director and ask him or her to demonstrate that they are staying within the parameters that the Board has set, talk with the staff and clients/patients/audience to make sure that they're getting what they need. This team should look over the books and ask questions. They should be out in the community asking people if they're happy that the non-profit is there. They should be talking with like organizations in other parts of the country to see what's being tried elsewhere and how it's going. So while the staff is dedicated to carrying out the Board's policies, the Board must be dedicated to making sure that the policies are relevant, visionary, on target and meeting the need. If they are not, it's time to change the policies.

4) **They represent the organization in the community.** Board members are your organization's ambassadors. At service club meetings, political functions, corporate gatherings and social

...rotating evaluation teams see that people are getting what they need, look at the books, and ask questions

...policies are relevant, visionary, on target, meeting the need

settings, it is important for your Board members to talk about the work your organization is doing. People in the community will judge your organization by the quality, standing and dedication of your vocal Board members. I recommend that organizations reinforce this important representational role by having business cards printed for each Board member with the logo, name and address of the non-profit along with the Board member's name and title (President, Fundraising Chair, Treasurer, etc.) Please avoid those tacky cards with a blank space for your Board member to write in his or her name. Spend the eighteen bucks and have it done right. It is very impressive to have your volunteers out there handing out your cards. Talk about dedication!

...the community will judge your organization by its Board

5) **And last, but certainly not least: It is the Board's responsibility to give and raise money.** There is not one sentence in the English language that will make a roomful of Board members dig their heels in deeper than that one. If that sentence were a horse, it would be a dead one from all of the times it's been trotted out and beaten. Here are my five best arguments for why it is the Board's RESPONSIBILITY to give and raise money:

It is the Board's responsibility to give and raise money.

❖ If the Board is setting policy and deciding what is going to happen for what people at what cost, by not raising the money to make it happen they are creating an impossible situation. If the Board decided to give the entire staff an 11% raise, but did nothing about finding the money to make it happen, not only would the staff not get their raise, but the

Board would be acting in a highly irresponsible manner and should all resign in disgrace for letting the organization down.

❖ Major donors, corporate givers and foundations are becoming more adamant about not giving until you have 100% giving from your Board members. Several foundations now require a list of your Board members and how much they give. If your own family/Board won't give, you cannot expect anyone else to give. As a matter of fact, I maintain that until every one of your Board members is giving to the absolute best of their ability, you have no business fundraising in the community.

...foundations often require a list of Board members and how much they give

Every time I talk about Board giving, people see lots of zeroes and commas. Please understand that I am NOT saying that you should have only big hitters on your Board. That would be a terrible disservice to your organization and to your community. What I am saying is that every Board member should give, not until it hurts, but until it feels really good. What I wish for your organization is that you have a Board full of people who put your organization first on their community priority list and the single largest gift they give each year is to you. For some people that might be $25. For others it might be $25,000,000,000,000. If it is the absolute most they can give, then the gifts are equal regardless of the number of zeroes each carries.

What I wish for your organization is that you have a Board full of people who have put you first on their community priority list.

❖ Everyone can give something. If you ask your monied Board members to give, and you do not ask your low income Board members to give for fear of embarrassing them, you are doing

...the gifts are equal regardless of the number of zeroes

281

elitist fundraising and insulting your low income volunteers. You are also creating two classes of Board members: those who are expected to give and those who are too poor. This kind of splitting of your Board will result in an imbalance of power that will haunt you when your givers start to think that their word carries more weight than that of your non-giving members. You are also saying that the Board members with money can give and be part of the dynamic growth of the organization, but the low income members are too poor to be part of the solution.

❖ If you have a Board that understands raising money but refuses to give because they give their "time", I suggest that you remind them that the phone company does not accept "time" instead of money when you pay your bill. I also suggest that it is very difficult to ask someone else to do something that you yourself are not willing to do. If someone came to you with tickets that they wanted you to buy for an upcoming event, but they were not planning to support the event, I doubt that you would be convinced to buy the tickets.

❖ Writing a check is an important part of real commitment. I believe it's called "putting your money where your mouth is." Once your Board members have their own money committed to the program, they've bought in. It's theirs. I recommend that one Board member be in charge of Board giving. This person will stand up once a year and say, "It's that time again. If I do not have your check or pledge by the end of this week, I will call you and make an appointment to talk about your

...the phone company does not accept "time" instead of money

It is very difficult to ask someone else to do something you are not willing to do.

Signing a check is an important part of real commitment.

gift." It helps if this person is exceptionally good with follow-through, and it helps if this person is someone that the Board members would rather not have to deal with in person so they just do it when instructed. If yours is a member organization, I recommend that you require Board members to pay the membership fee and make a gift on top of that.

Board Development

If these five areas of responsibility are news to you and you would like to move your Board toward functioning in these ways, one key tool for change is the nominating process, in conjunction with enforcing the terms of office.

The length of tenure for your Board members is spelled out in your By-Laws. It usually calls for two two-year or three-year terms. If you enforce the terms of office, you must state in the By-Laws that no person may serve more than the prescribed amount of time. If you are not enforcing the terms, then the terms mean nothing. People just keep renewing their terms of office over and over, and that makes it very difficult to move dead wood out and new energy in. Enforcing terms of office gives your organization the opportunity to renew itself. If everyone moves on when their term expires, then you have gracious exits and no hurt feelings. The dead-wood folks get their letter of thanks and no more need be said. The energetic, follow-through folks can be recycled onto a committee as a community representative and a year later asked to join the

...enforcing terms of office

283

Board again for a new term.

The words "hurt feelings" are, in fact, a mine field, and more than one non-profit has blown itself up there. The fear of hurting peoples' feelings makes organizations hold onto destructive volunteers, or make convoluted plans based on whose feelings are in the way, and can actually stop all forward progress while a fragile ego is being cared for. We all love the non-profit world because it is full of caring people. But please do not lose sight of the need for your organization to go forward. And remember that your mission statement does not include sacrificing the health and well-being of your organization to avoid hurting someone's feelings.

Many years ago I worked with a non-profit organization that was losing $30,000 per year. They were on the downhill slide and morale was very low. The Board decided that the only thing to do was to sell the very grand building that they owned and occupied. Their program was not dependent on the building at all. It just served as their office and the program took place elsewhere. Four volunteers did not like that decision. They met and plotted and decided to have the building declared a landmark worthy of protection from sale. They petitioned, lobbied and generally made a great fuss over this building. The morale of the organization sunk to an all-time low. Everything stopped. All energy focused on the "gang of four". These four folks prepared a strategy for raising the needed $30,000 per year that included, as I remember, bake sales and car washes. The Board hired me to review the strategy, review the decision to sell

Your mission statement does not include sacrificing the health of your organization to avoid hurting someone's feelings.

284

the building, and make a recommendation to them. I talked to some objective third parties from around the country, reviewed all of the documents and advised the Board to ignore the gang of four and proceed with the sale. I mediated the confrontation between the dissidents and the Board, each side had their say, and the sale eventually went through. But I remain amazed at the fuss kicked up by four people. The Board had the obligation to listen to their argument, but in the name of not hurting their feelings, they spent inordinate amounts of time and money to mollify four very loud people.

If you have to step on some toes, say you're sorry, but keep moving forward.

Moving people out is part one. Moving people in is part two. Finding the right people is an on-going process that requires an active, inventive, energetic nominating committee. The way nominating committees usually work goes something like this: there's a Board meeting and the President notices that there's an empty chair. He or she says, "We need a warm body to sit there. Would someone like to volunteer to find someone?" Every head drops, as the entire Board suddenly becomes fascinated with the Treasurer's Report. The first person to look up becomes the nominating committee. This person goes out and says to her or his buddy, "**Please** be on my Board! You won't have to do anything." (Then the Board wonders why this new person isn't doing anything.)

The nominating committee should:

The first person to look up becomes the Nominating Committee.

* Meet year-round
* Work from the Long Range Plan to identify skills that will be needed in the coming years.
* Be the best and the brightest of the group
* Be willing to literally cold call, interview and keep track of potential Board members.
* Be enthusiastic, positive, and honest about the organization
* Be ad hoc, with everyone on the Board getting the chance to rotate through.
* Include the Director of Development as a full-fledged member.

The nominating committee does not invite anyone to be on the Board. That is the responsibility and privilege of the entire Board. The job of the nominating committee is to build a waiting list for Board membership that the Board will use to choose new members when terms expire.

How to Build a Board Waiting List

A waiting list for Board membership is a list of people who have been interviewed by the nominating committee and have clearly stated their interest in serving on the Board at some future date. Skills, interest levels and details of the interviews are all noted confidentially and the list is reviewed by the Board when they know that a vacancy is about to occur.

An active, inventive, energetic committee builds a waiting list that the Board will use to choose new members as terms expire.

The waiting list serves several functions:

First, it allows the nominating committee to interview people without having to commit to asking them to join. It has happened that someone seems like the perfect candidate, but turns out to be a perfect turkey. It is very awkward, at the end of the interview, to say, "Wow, I had no idea what a jerk you are. Never mind." Instead, everyone who is interested is invited to be added to the waiting list. The committee or interviewer explains that they do not have the power to invite anyone to be on the Board, and that people are chosen from the waiting list based on what skills are needed at the moment.

The waiting list lets you interview people without having to ask them to join.

Second, the waiting list serves to keep your Board members on their toes. I am always appalled when an utterly inactive Board member says to me, "I would resign, but I don't want to leave them in the lurch." (Please! Leave them in the lurch!) The waiting list exists to remind Board members that there are many excellent people waiting to sit in their seat.

...there are many excellent people waiting for a turn

And **last** but not least, the waiting list energizes the organization. Rather than taking the "warm body" approach to Board development, the waiting list process is a constant reminder that you are loved and important.

The nominating committee starts with the Long Range Plan. Suppose your organization has decided that next year they will start to explore the possibility of raising money for an educational program. They know that they will need to add three specialists to the staff, beef up the public relations, and raise an additional $100,000 for the project. They will need a satellite office in the downtown area, and they will need the cooperation of the school district. All of that is in the Plan. The nominating committee then sets to work on filling in the names and faces of the people who can make that happen. First, they start with the skills:

-fundraising
-school liaison
-downtown realtor
-downtown merchant/mover and shaker
-connections to a P.R. firm
-maybe a futurist in your field
-maybe a high-profile educator to give the project credibility
-local politicians

This list then goes back to the Board to play "Who do you Know?" The best way to flesh out this list is to brainstorm. Write down every name that is suggested. Those names will spark other names. Pretty soon you will have a long list of possibilities. Talk about them. Who on the list would be super to get on the Board? Who would be easy/difficult to work with? Who knows whom well enough to open the door for the nominating committee? Prioritize the list.

Starting with your number one, the nominating committee will approach the prospects. If you do not know the prospect well, write a letter first. Tell the prospect who you are, what the organization does, what is expected of a Board member, and how their name came into nomination. Do not be afraid to say,

...play "Who do you Know?"

Never be afraid to say: "We have a plan, this is where you fit into the plan, and we need you for your special skills and contacts."

"We have a Plan, this is where you fit in the Plan, and we need you for your special skills and contacts." Tell the prospect that you will call on Tuesday, then call on Tuesday. When you call, you are not discussing Board membership. You are calling to make an appointment to interview the candidate in person.

If you get the appointment, remember that this means the prospect is interested. At the appointment, it is the interviewer's job to represent the organization and the Board totally honestly. Tell it all. When I was Chair of Major Gifts for the Mill Valley Schools Community Foundation, the nominating committee found us a great asker, a man who was very skilled in business, full of personality, and well-connected. He called me to talk about the amount of time required for the Board and committee work, and I told him that it would be the most demanding volunteer work he could ever imagine. There was a long pause, but he eventually agreed. If I had down-played the time and commitment required, either it would have taken me a very long time to bring him up to speed, or he would most likely have quit as soon as he realized that I deceived him.

The nominating committee members are looking for specific skills. They must also keep their eyes open for people who fit in with the "family" of the Board, people with the energy and personalities, and certainly the sense of humor, to match the present mix of people. And they must keep in mind that the Board, and the organization, will be infinitely richer if they aim for a rich mixture of people by profession, ethnicity, sex and everything else. I once worked for an organization whose Board

If you get the appointment, the prospect is interested.

was made up of lawyers, judges, and social workers. When the nominating committee went out to find new members, they came back with lawyers, judges and social workers. Make sure that your nominating committee is willing to stretch themselves and call on people they do not know but who could be of service to the Board.

Welcoming New Board Talent

Once the new members come on board, I recommend that you give them the opportunity to hit the ground running. I have talked to Board members who refer to themselves as "new", and then it turns out that they've been on the Board for a year! The rules for plugging in new Board members are:

1) Recruit them for a specific reason, and then work with them to set their information, contacts and ideas directly into motion;

2) Try the Buddy System. Assign each new Board member to a seasoned veteran. They should ride to and from the meetings together, and sit next to each other at meetings. It is often difficult for a new member to raise his or her hand to ask what might be a stupid question. The question can be answered off to the side by the Buddy. The Buddy can also fill in the blanks: who always disagrees with whom, who likes to talk, who is best friends with whom, etc.

3) Orientation, on-going training, and yearly retreats are essential. No matter how many Boards your new members have sat on, it is imperative that you sit the new members down

Help them hit the ground running.

...the Buddy fills in the blanks

Ongoing training is in your own best interest.

with all of the information your organization has to offer and explain in great detail how the programs work and what the books look like. Give them a detailed history of your organization. Some organizations even require that new Board members attend the volunteer training so that they can have a hands-on sense of how the programs work. On-going training can be in your own best interest: the information and increased awareness you give the Board will make your Board feel better prepared to get the organization's work done. This is a great way to use a consultant who knows Boards and can give them new ideas and energy. It can also make the Board feel important and well cared for. And the yearly retreat is a unique opportunity for the Board to bond. They socialize, play ping pong, and get work done without disturbances. Retreat time is good for reviewing and modifying the Plan, recommitting to the goals, and carrying on the folk lore of the organization. At the Retreat, either hire an outside facilitator or set up skilled Board members to each lead a section of the agenda.

...the yearly retreat is a unique opportunity

Boards and Leadership

People change because they want to or need to. It is a frustrating part of being a human being that we cannot CHANGE others, no matter how good our argument is for why they should change. If only everyone would do everything we wanted them to do, wouldn't this world be a much better place?

Good arguments, cajoling and pleading do little to move Boards to do what needs to be done. When a Board has functioned by letting people off the hook, never enforcing terms of office, and asking nothing more than attendance at meetings, it is a huge task to now ask them to WORK. And it is even harder to ask them to take responsibility for the planning they've done and go out and find the money to make the plans happen. The key ingredient for this kind of formidable movement is leadership.

A leader is someone who can inspire people to do what the leader knows needs to be done. A leader can overcome his or her fear of not being liked to say what needs to be said. A leader holds people to their word, reminds them of their commitment and moves them to act by setting a great example. If a leader wants 10 hours from a volunteer, she or he gives 30. It helps if the leader knows how to run a tight meeting -- moving items on the agenda, dealing with the people who like to pontificate, and holding more or less to the agreed rules of order with humor and grace.

It is very difficult to teach someone how to lead. It is like trying to teach someone how to write: it helps tremendously if there's some inclination there from the beginning. If a Board is struggling with lack of leadership, I recommend that the nominating committee focus on **recruiting** someone with leadership skills to be the Board President. This may sound like heresy, but the logic is simple: It is difficult to take someone who knows everything about you and teach that person how to lead and inspire others. It is easier to take someone who has exhibited leadership skills and teach them everything they need to know about your organization. I also recommend at the same time having your most skilled in-house leader serve as Vice President for a year under the new President with the idea that that person will take over as President at the end of her or his apprenticeship. If you institute this "learning" time for upcoming Board Presidents, you will be giving those volunteers new leadership skills that they would get nowhere else.

The Board leader's main job is to build the team and move it forward. This is a very selfless act. It requires that the leader put aside his or her agendas and ego and act for the good of the organization.

A good leader puts aside his own agenda and ego, and acts for the good of the organization.

I recently met a woman who was the President of a Board in transition. The Founder of the organization had just died, and during his life he had been the kind of person who just quietly paid the bills and ran the ship based on his vision. Without him, they were helpless children. Two camps of people arose, each with their own righteous visions of where the organization needed to go. This woman, instead of siding with one or the other, took a mediation role. The debate became, at times, almost violent. She felt as if she were being torn apart, but she stuck with it, letting both sides be heard. Finally, one camp prevailed, the other retreated, and the organization went forward with creating a cohesive five year plan. Her leadership saw the organization through in an almost invisible way.

Founder's Syndrome

So it must be said that leadership does not mean imposing your own agenda, intimidating people, or railroading meetings. The

293

central issue for a team is trusting the person who is calling the plays and doing your own part exquisitely, whether it's a starring role or not. The best thing that can happen for any Board is achieving 100% agreement. If you have 100% agreement as your goal, whether it's agreement on fundraising or program planning or whatever, you will always be striving for the best. Be careful of settling for anything less. Of course 100% of anything is difficult. But as soon as you shrug your shoulders and start letting people off the hook for any reason, you will slide into mediocrity. Why not continue to work toward 100%? It's a worthwhile goal, and it is reachable.

As soon as you let people off the hook, you will slide into mediocrity.

In addition to inspiring people and building the team, there is the very mundane issue of having a leader who knows how to run a good meeting. Here are some rules for running a meeting:

1) No unnecessary meetings. Do not meet to exchange information. Do that kind of informing in writing. Meet to bring together the chemistry of the people to create something new. Meet to make important decisions.

...no unnecessary meetings

2) Always begin and end on time. If the leader sets the pace for this, eventually people will stop saying, "Oh, they never start on time," shooting to arrive at the meeting 20 minutes late.

Start and end on time.

3) No meetings over 90 minutes. If you can't do it in 90 minutes, you'll need to call another meeting.

4) If you're having trouble with #3, try setting time limits to each agenda item. Assign a time keeper. Ask each person who has an item to present on the agenda how long it will take. Cut off pontificating with responses like, "I think that we've heard all of

the issues. Is there a new issue anyone would like to bring up?" or "Would someone like to call the question?" And if the discussion goes beyond the time limit, either take it up at the next meeting or send it to an ad hoc committee for clarification or further research.

5) Do not ask people to meet to discuss anything that they cannot take action on. I recently spoke with a friend who landed the Executive Director job at a very large, very political non-profit. At one point in the very long hiring process the Board committee asked my friend to attend a staff meeting as some kind of informal interview. She asked, "Will they have any say in the hiring?" When the Board member responded in the negative, she declined to attend, telling the Board member, "That's an impossible situation for the staff. If they have no power, don't give them mixed signals by asking their advice and then not taking it. I'll meet the staff after I'm hired." The moral of the story is, if they don't get to decide how it will be, don't ask them to review how it's going.

In addition to these rules, I have two recommendations for the smooth running of a Board. The first is to have the Board sit down once a year, preferably at the retreat, and develop 11 or 12 agendas for the coming year. If you are following my train of thought about having evaluation take place outside of Board meetings, then the need for discussing the financial statement and Executive Director's report disappears. That is done by small evaluation teams and briefly reported back to the Board, unless they uncover a big problem that needs attention. Freed from these burdens, the Board then can get to the meat of the

If they don't get to decide how it will be, don't ask them to review how it's going.

Develop 11 or 12 agendas for the coming year.

work at hand. They can pull back and see what they need to learn, and where the organization needs to grow. So suppose that, at the retreat, the Board decides that more exposure in the community is the organization's most pressing need. They can then plan three or four one-hour sessions to help attract more exposure for the organization. So they might decide, for the first meeting after the retreat, to call in the PR person and several key program people and start to explore what's been done and what's new and exciting in the programs that might merit media coverage. At the next meeting they might invite the local newspaper publisher, the local radio station manager, and a friend who owns an ad agency to meet with them and the PR staff person to brainstorm ways to get more exposure. At the third meeting they might focus all of their efforts on working with the nominating committee to brainstorm names of people who can help meet exposure goals for the coming three years. Finally, they might create ad hoc committees to call similar organizations around the country to see what they're doing to create more community exposure. This is a more creative approach than endlessly reviewing financial statements, complaining about how much is being spent on Rotary Club dues, and worrying about why the years fly by and no one is doing anything about increasing PR.

Committees

The second piece of advice has to do with your committee structure. If it is working perfectly, let it be. But if people go

onto committees and are never heard from again, you may want to think about doing committees differently. I recommend abolishing "standing" committees. You will notice that they are not called "running" committees. People are generally assigned to a committee like PR, finance, programs, or fundraising not necessarily because of any burning desire to work in any of these areas, but because the committee exists and it needs people. When a problem arises that needs attention, the President sends it "to committee". I have found that the people "on committee" are not always the best people to solve the problem. Suppose, for instance, that the staff wants a better benefit package. The Executive Director brings the problem to the Board and the President refers the issue to the Finance Committee for review. The Finance Committee is two C.P.A.'s and a Loan Officer. They look at the question and say, "We can't afford it." A more creative approach would have been to look not only at the cost but at the way other similar-sized non-profits are offering benefits, and at creative ways to offer incentives. That would require more and different skills, perhaps, than just the Finance Committee has.

Eliminate the Fundraising Committee. I have noticed that most of the people who were assigned to the fundraising committee, especially the chair of that committee, were not in the room when the appointment was made. I have met literally hundreds of chairs of fundraising who hate the idea of asking for money. Another argument against standing committees is that they are often trying to do work that is usually a staff function, or they are trying to do work that is more properly the job of the entire

Long-range planning, budgeting, and fundraising are not committee material.

Board. Long range planning, budgeting, and fundraising, for instance, are not committee assignments. They are the responsibility of the whole Board. Working on small parts of either of these tasks is appropriate, such as researching deferred giving programs or interviewing similar organizations about their long range plans. But that information is then fed back to the whole Board for action. In like manner, when a fundraising committee exists and the organization starts running out of money, the Board tends to point a finger at the fundraising committee and ask, "Well, what have you been doing?" Raising money and identifying funding sources are the work of the entire Board.

The best way to approach committee structure is on an ad hoc basis. This requires very strong leadership, so please make sure that you have a very effective President before you institute an ad hoc approach. The way this works is very simple. The President initiates and dissolves committees as needed. So instead of a fundraising committee, there is a chair of fundraising who is a person who LIKES FUNDRAISING! This person works with the Director of Development, if there is one, to draw up a draft of the fundraising plan for the coming year, including activities with both money and people goals. The Chair then meets with each Board member, explains the plan, solicits comment, and asks each Board member to plug into one activity for the year. If the person is a corporate executive, that person would probably plug into the corporate campaign. Once he or she has picked their activity for the year, that person is not asked to sell raffle tickets, blow up balloons or lick postage

...the power of ad hoc committees

stamps. That person goes off and totally focuses on the corporate campaign. When it is over, his or her fundraising responsibilities are met for the year. In this way, everyone is not caught up in a constant state of fundraising. Each Board member can contribute to the fundraising effort to the best of their ability, and when it's over they take a break from fundraising until next year.

In terms of the day-to-day work of the Board, the ad hoc approach makes even more sense. In the example of the organization that will focus on PR in the coming year, the President is faced with an amorphous "research" job. If there were a standing committee system in place, the President would have to choose which committee could handle the job. Would it be Program? Finance? Or there might even be a PR committee to handle it. But suppose that the PR committee members had never done research? If they are assigned the research task because it seems like the most appropriate committee to do the work, chances are that the task will sit there and never get done. You would be amazed at how many committees of non-profit Boards receive an assignment about which they know nothing. Some struggle to complete it, some stop attending meetings. In either case, it leaves a bad taste in the mouth. In the ad hoc model, when a job arises that would be best handled by a committee, the President knows the skills and follow-through records of the Board members. So she might say, "John, would you head this research project?" Now remember, John is not burdened with standing committee meetings, and the President knows that this is the kind of project John likes, so he just might

You would be amazed at how many committees receive assignments about which they know nothing.

299

say yes. Then she asks for volunteers, just two or three, to work with John. "When can you have this information for us?" she asks John. One month, two months, however he responds, he knows that she will hold him to that deadline. So John and his committee complete the research as assigned, and they report back to the Board with the information: "In Tucson, there's a Wellness group that has printed a great brochure for the business community. Here are copies for you. We think that we should follow their lead in our community." At this point, three things are happening:

1) The Board has the information they wanted, so they feel satisfied.

2) John and his committee have completed their assignment. They are praised for work well done, so they feel very satisfied.

3) John and his committee are done. They are now free for another assignment, which they are likely to get because they followed through, and they are likely to accept another assignment because they feel appreciated.

...they are likely to accept another assignment because they feel appreciated

This ad hoc approach also helps create a more participatory atmosphere. Board members see other Board members volunteering, following through and being thanked. Soon a "this is how we work here" attitude develops. Where you're going with this is toward a Board full of people who wouldn't dream of coming to a meeting and confessing, "I didn't follow through."

"This is how we work here."

300

Living in the Future

As your Board members think through their roles in the non-profit, it is important that they realize it is their job to live in the future.

Picture your organization as a giant stone wheel that constantly rolls slowly forward. The Board, in my experience, is usually running behind this wheel putting out fires. First there's not enough money to meet payroll. Oh No! "Everyone come help put out this fire!" Then there's the leaky roof. Oh No! "Everyone! Hurry! There's another fire!" In the meantime, that wheel just keeps rolling somewhere. Often, somewhere down the road, the Board stops putting out fires long enough to notice that the wheel is in the gutter and the organization is obsolete.

Where the Board should be is out front. If they have determined where the organization needs to be in five or ten years, and they have hired a professional to run the organization day to day, then they can be constantly looking ahead to where that wheel needs to go to have it be on the right track.

If you have a Board that loves to diddle with the details, getting drawn into staff feuds, spending endless hours deciding what the logo will look like, arguing issues that have already been settled, they are not living in the future. The problem here is that if the Board doesn't take care of the future, no one will. The staff is busy taking care of the present.

If the Board doesn't take care of the future, no one will.

When your organization is given tax-exempt status, this means that it holds a special place in the fabric of your community. It means that your organization exists to meet a need or solve a problem. That is how we are different from for-profit businesses. Non-profits arise to answer a need that already exists. If the need goes away, then the non-profit is free to go and solve another problem elsewhere. Since the need arises from the community, that makes the community the rightful owner of the non-profits that exist to help the community meet its own needs.

...the community is the owner

The Board is the keeper of the vision. They are acting in the name of the community to make your organization the absolute best it can be. They must answer to the community for the decisions they make. This includes creating a viable plan that will ensure the health of your organization into the next decade. It means recruiting and challenging the absolute best team of Board members you can find. It means continually making sure that your organization is meeting the need it claims to address.

...the Board is the "Keeper of the Vision"

We are all temporary caretakers of the non-profits we serve. We come for a time, leave our mark, for good or bad, on the work they do, and we go away, leaving that work to the next generation. So while you serve, you have the chance to use your stewardship as a Board member in the most visionary way possible. Putting out fires is the least creative way to spend your Board time. Envisioning the organization as the best and the brightest, and then helping to move it forward to make that happen, is the most creative.

We are all temporary caretakers of the non-profits we serve.

Conclusion

In conclusion, I bring you the Keegan and Galley Two-Step Program to Fundraising and Board Development:

1) Get over it.

2) Get on with it.

Whatever is stopping you from getting on with it is very real. Working for non-profits is like raising children. There's more heart in it than any other job you could possibly choose. But when you come to that job with love and you care very much, you've got to be ready to have your heart broken a little, too. And, of course, at this moment you have three options. You can go back to your organization and live with all its faults because you still have something to learn from the experience. Or you can stand up and speak out for change, chancing that people will not like you, even chancing losing your job. Or you can get out.

Wherever you are stuck, it is probably temporary. If it is not temporary, scrap the whole thing and take your talents elsewhere. Life is too short. If it is temporary, take a deep breath and think about what you would do if your organization were the first priority in your life for, say, the next six months. What four really great things could you make happen for them and for you? What one thing can you make happen TODAY to bring some excellence to the work your organization is doing in the community? This will not solve all of your problems, but the time to take one step forward is right now.

About the Author

P. Burke Keegan is a teacher of all aspects of Fundraising and Board Development. She spent the first six years of her fundraising career working for grassroots social service organizations in Southern California--producing special events, writing grants and direct mail, going on major gifts and corporate asks, and conducting membership drives. The next phase of her career found her traveling and teaching the five-day fundraising course for the Grantsmanship Center out of Los Angeles. In 1982 she settled in Marin County, California and built her consulting and teaching practice. In that capacity she has worked with organizations such as St. Vincent de Paul Society, Marin Abused Women's Services, The San Jose Cleveland Ballet, California NOW, and the Chinese Community Housing Corporation. She also has traveled extensively presenting seminars on Fundraising and Board Development to organizations such as United Way of Sacramento, Association of California Symphony Orchestras, California Consortium of Education Foundations, Goodwill Industries Volunteers and the Georgia Assembly of Arts Organizations. She served on the faculty of Golden Gate University in San Francisco for five years teaching Fundraising to Arts Administration graduate students, and has taught for the University of San Francisco in the Rehabilitation Administration graduate program.

Partners Press
518D Tamalpais Dr., Ste. 60
Corte Madera, CA 94925

(415) 381-5290
FAX: (415) 491-4639

For each copy, enclose a check or money order for $20.00 PLUS $2.00 per book for postage and handling.

Total amount enclosed: $_____

Please make checks payable to "P. Burke Keegan"

_____ I cannot wait 3-4 weeks for Book Rate. Here is $3.00 additional per book for Air Mail.

Name: ....

Organization: ....

Title: ....

Address: ....

.... Zip: ....

Daytime Phone: ....

Partners Press
518D Tamalpais Dr., Ste. 60
Corte Madera, CA 94925

(415) 381-5290
FAX: (415) 491-4639

For each copy, enclose a check or money order for $20.00 PLUS $2.00 per book for postage and handling.

Total amount enclosed: $_____

Please make checks payable to "P. Burke Keegan"

_____ I cannot wait 3-4 weeks for Book Rate. Here is $3.00 additional per book for Air Mail.

Name: ....

Organization: ....

Title: ....

Address: ....

.... Zip: ....

Daytime Phone: ....

Partners Press
518D Tamalpais Dr., Ste. 60
Corte Madera, CA 94925

(415) 381-5290
FAX: (415) 491-4639

For each copy, enclose a check or money order for $20.00 PLUS $2.00
per book for postage and handling.

Total amount enclosed: $_____

Please make checks payable to "P. Burke Keegan"

_____ I cannot wait 3-4 weeks for Book Rate. Here is $3.00
additional per book for Air Mail.

Name: ....

Organization: ....

Title: ....

Address: ....

.... Zip: ....

Daytime Phone: ....